LEVEN BETTS : PATTERN RECOGNITION

D1592880

# LEVEN BETTS : PATTERN RECOGNITION

David Leven and Stella Betts

Introduction by Michael Sorkin

GRAHAM FOUNDATION FOR ADVANCED STUDIES IN THE FINE ARTS, CHICAGO

PRINCETON ARCHITECTURAL PRESS, NEW YORK

# Contents

# Letter to Dave and Stella

Michael Sorkin

Dear Dave and Stella,

I am writing you a letter so that a little introduction won't turn into a conclusion or an epitaph. A monograph is a kind of debut, after all, and you cannot help but have a future filled with promise: you are remarkably talented and have plenty of time. Nevertheless, you should, I think, avoid making too many promises to yourselves.

A couple of reasons for this. First, you must reserve the right to make dramatic, even eccentric, changes in your work. There is a professional trajectory that we're all familiar with: an architect starts out modestly, establishes a legible style, and proceeds incrementally to build a practice. A monograph can serve as a progress report for such a course. It will, however, fix you in the professional gaze at one point in your careers. You must be careful that it doesn't fix your own investigation, as it has with so many architects who have matured prematurely.

A monograph can also be something a little more aggressive, polemical, irritating. The model here is Le Corbusier, who was constantly tossing off little books filled with architectural propositions in an attempt to place his project in a revolutionary context and to bloat his taste with big meaning. While some deliberate association with larger constructs may be unavoidable, the production of monographs is always contextual. Some, by focusing on the local tectonics of built work, attempt to occupy a space outside of—above—association; ritual purifications of the formal. Others take a more patently polemical tack in which the object yields to the ideas it purportedly embodies. Your book strides the fine line between realized work and propositions. This figures in the gap opened between your lapidary domestic and gallery work and the large-scale theoretical projects that lift this book so far above the everyday. Your Wetland City, Filter Park, and Spaces Between the Hills studies are brilliant inhabitations of the borderland between necessity and desire. The physically scoured but socially laden slate of New Orleans East is one of those accidentally amazing sites, demanding action and desperately in need of re-imagination, of mental invention, of recovery into circumstances forever changed. So too the hills of Jerusalem and the streets of Chicago.

Like the Filter Parking studies these projects grow from an idea about infrastructure. Current interest in such nominally "neutral" construction offers a way of dealing with the city at a scale that comes to grips with the immensity of the problems it confronts, a way around the strictures of both megalomania and the "everyday." Hurricanes, massive flooding, the automobile, air pollution, racism: all are subjects for your research, and you have been very canny about the scale of your attack. Your Filter Parking projects, for example, are not shy about the generic modularity of parking lots and understand the way in which they create a universal "sited-ness" that always begs some form of architectural and environmental attenuation.

Your scheme for New Orleans—Wetland City—takes the ravished particularity of the post-Katrina city's east side to make a proposition that is simultaneously local and abstract. Its optimism—and political vigor—grow from your insistence that the devastated community be rehoused in place and that the armature for that reconstruction be a set of transportation links back to the city center. Its big infrastructure does not shy from extensive construction. The way you juxtapose this logical expenditure to such failed projects as the Mississippi River Gulf Outlet (the notorious "Mr. Go") calibrates its logic as settlement as clearly as the inclusion of the Wetlands International Protection Institute (WIPI) suggests that a balance of building and "nature" is not simply a withdrawal of the former from the latter.

When I looked at a draft of your book, these big, polemically minded projects came at the end, your essay "Pattern Recognition" at the front. The linear interplay of principles, corroboration, and culmination yields a most interesting intra-textual discourse. For example, because both the Filter Parking garage in Chicago and the New Orleans project have enough architectonic form to wrap the membranes of style and organization, your precise work at smaller scales, including your extremely lovely built projects, fills in the gaps in the more liminal polemic of forms left carefully underdeveloped for the sake of argument. These are gaps that include both density and, for want of a better word, style.

Your security and precision as designers and the clarity of your taste have led you to what is, I think, an appropriate caution about making the architectural prosody of these projects too specific. I know I believe in the diagram of the Wetland City with its low-rise, dense-enough-looking street spines. Nothing about the representations you offer suggests either the impossibility of urbanity or—when the architecture gets ratcheted up—that the predomination of your own taste and form, applied in appropriate measure and scale, would fail to yield the desired effect. That you lay back is a marker both of the sincerity of your political intentions and of your extremely canny sense of where to invest the descriptive oomph in your advocacy.

Can you have a monograph without an apologia, some form of the architectural-procedural? Probably not. I remember agonizing over this when I did my first monograph during a theory-burdened time. I wanted the work to "speak for itself" and wound up making a book that was probably too parsimonious with explanation and too image-driven. To be sure, we architects remain overcommitted to the idea that the theoretical must inhabit the realm of the philosophical, and we've given short shrift to other strategies of account. The too-reticent engagement of the profession with the social and the environmental is, in part, a by-product of this distorting mislocation. Your work resists this in the clarity of its concerns and through a process that uses serviceable logics of place, proportion, construction, and the phenomenal to establish both order and identity. You trust yourselves and your experience, and this confidence is never misplaced.

Still, you've gone to pains to produce a theoretical account of your work. The danger, always, is that the theory is a retrofit, a longing for some authenticating inscription that may or may not have any operational consequence. Your idea of "pattern recognition" is extremely astute in this way. The concept suggests a series of inherencies or imminencies, something already there that can be unraveled by shifts in perspective, by decoding and inference, by the delamination of layers of intervention by other actors, other sensibilities. Cognitive, it also suggests the arbitrary quality of the imposition, its dependence on willful observation, on the taste and capacity of the observer. The theory asserts your responsiveness to context as well as your insistence on a non-formulaic mode of absorbing it. You argue for shifting perspectives, the idea that neither angels nor ants can get the whole picture.

In your work, your recognition and manipulation of pattern becomes both structural and casual. Your patterns are lexical but not universal. It may be that your analogy with the routines of artificial intelligence pushes too far, but it is surely useful in this sense: it suggests that there is a real boundary between pattern recognition and pattern imposition. You write about your use of this analytic instrument as "intention laden," and this is crucial. In distinguishing your work from the protest-too-much avatars of "scripted" solutions, you are not shy about your insistence on transparency between what is programmed—intended—and what is observed and lived. Your insistence on the intentionality—the intelligence—behind your methodologies at once establishes a conscience for architecture and makes an important place for the idea of the natural in your work.

Part of the charm of AI and of parametric strategies in architectural design is that they appear "natural" precisely because of their claims to a kind of machine autonomy. At this early moment in the transition from carbon- to silicon-based intelligence, much of the appeal of computational architecture is in the complex, apparently "neural" patterning of the looping and accumulating recalculation that produces forms, in theory departing by increments from their originating program. Of course, conventional intelligence must always be applied at the back end of such strategies when, quick as a wink, the architect recognizes that the door is too small to admit human bodies, that the thing is unbuildable, or simply that it doesn't look good. Automation is not yet able to trump such judgments, nor should it. The clarity of your recognition that pattern is simply a tool for formal invention, for analysis of context(s), and for testing and incorporating known facts or hypotheses allows you to escape the inflated notions of the "natural" that seem to accompany so much of the rhetoric of parametric design.

This claim is in many ways bizarre but also familiar. Certainly, it is part of a discourse that has many of its monuments in the Frankenstein tradition, and in the anxiety formed at the hubristic juncture between the idea that nature is ours to control and invent and the idea that we are not exceptional, that nature is something we can never stand outside of. And architecture's participation in the natural world is greatly foregrounded these days by what has become the most active site of the architectural conscience: the environment, a word that now substitutes for *nature*. What distinguishes your work is that you are so acutely conscious of the act of yourselves viewing, that you acknowledge (and pride in) your own prejudices, convictions, and tastes, and that you do not insist that your analysis or methodology affords your work any special authority—that is, no authority beyond what is literally present in the work. This critical relationship to the utility of the theoretical will save you from the risk that theory will annihilate the possibility of continuing.

You sum up this process—your relationship to your own methodology—with the nice, strategically fuzzy phrase: the "informal formal." I like this because it reflects the refreshing fact that you're not full of yourselves, because it describes the idea of methodology's limits, because it reserves judgment, and because it so well describes a process—design—that is in constant oscillation between the regimes of regulation and spontaneity. Indeed, if I were seeking to sum up the work you've done to date, I would certainly have to include this very description, the idea of the constant reframing of conceptual armatures that are themselves subject to continuous and shifting forms of interrogation. In the ongoing construction of this dialectical edifice, you have been able to astutely observe the emergence of your own pattern, the series of consistencies that make your project your own.

As Dave and I know from the City College commencements we've attended together, our senior senator, Charles Schumer, delivers the same address every year, flabbergasting faculty with his serial *chutzpah*. Students, however, hearing it for the first time, are invariably charmed by the anecdote at its core about making the wrong choice between a fellowship and a girlfriend. And I presume they are heartened by the exuberance of the punch line: "Go for it!" What a great position you are in to take this advice. You are talented, brilliant, curious, driven, open-minded, and dedicated to both the artistic and the social. I look forward to years of watching your work grow richer and deeper.

Go for it!

Love,
Michael

# Pattern Recognition

David Leven and Stella Betts

Pattern recognition at 20,000 feet

Recently, from a vantage point of twenty thousand feet above the ground, on a flight back to New York from an out-of-town teaching gig, we looked out the plane window and watched a river switchback through a valley with a road running alongside it. The river curved naturally and repeatedly, while the road measured its path, approximating distances from the bank, refining the radii of curves for automobile movement, and straightening out whenever possible to cut efficiently through the topography of the gulch. Also visible were towns, neighborhoods, farms, industrial buildings, more roads, hills, valleys, etc. The fascination of seeing these built and natural formations from above—as anyone who has ever looked out a plane window knows—is that they become abstract and reveal flat and three-dimensional patterns that are imperceptible from the ground. As architects whose work and focus looks toward the urban, we can speculate from that distance what the patterns reveal about the geography; but to determine the underlying forces that formed these systems, we have to touch down, analyze details, and then go back up from time to time, to keep an eye on the big picture. This back-and-forth investigation speaks to the initial analytic phase in an active, open, intention-driven operation whose ultimate goal is the design of architecture and urban propositions. We call this inceptive phase "pattern recognition."

In this text, the term and its associated operative methods frame a presentation of the way we have made architecture during the first ten years of our practice. We use it to explain various organizational, conceptual, and formal tendencies, as well as methods of production, in our work. Pattern recognition, as an overall design process, is non-formulaic, and addresses all scales and positions of our work within the larger forces at play in architecture.

As architects, we confront massive amounts of material and information in the construction of buildings. In addition, technology is ever changing, while the desire for the inhabitation and performance of buildings is increasing—and the oil's running out and the planet's getting warmer. These are big challenges for the way buildings are conceived and produced. In that it enables us to confront all of these challenges, pattern recognition is our way forward through any type or scope of problem. Analytical in nature, it zeroes in on underlying organizations and teases out nonpreconceived alternatives by filtering, sorting, and sifting until something provocative emerges and kick-starts a design.

To begin, we often look for design potentials in the organizational systems of site, program, infrastructure, and technology. We see the road that follows the river as an analog to pattern recognition in that it is an imprint of all natural and designed determinants—geological, climatic, economic, political, engineered, and constructive—that inform its path and connections. And in order to apprehend these multivalent conditions and, ultimately, to design with them, we need pattern recognition to operate like Google Earth's "zoom" command: enhancing, sharpening, blurring, or pixelating the materials at hand, thereby extracting information that can be used to produce architectural solutions. Once distilled from the mix of incipient formations, these patterns are used to formulate diagrams, which are malleable, able to scale up and down, morph, and extend, in order to address the specifics of an architectural problem.

The configurations that we determine are not without relative intelligence or utility to a design problem. It is critical to ascertain the comparative levels of embedded intelligence in a particular condition at the outset of a pattern-recognition process. Intelligence, by this definition, is integrated, connected, and cognizant of natural and built potentials. Looking through the plane window at the road sparks a series of questions: Do the configurations of roads, buildings, farming, and landscape that we see from the air reveal a built logic that addresses the needs of the surrounding community and of the natural environment? Or are they short-term solutions that will have to be reconfigured later? Is the road well conceived in its implementation, construction, and connection of places, or does it wash out in storms or bypass communities in need of access? What determines the dimension and scale of the built components along the road? How might these determining factors change as the environment, technology, and the development of buildings and cities changes? And how might we propose intelligent ways of addressing these questions? As architects, we strive to unpack these questions so that we can implement an intelligence of site or of program. Without a close analysis that asks questions and confronts norms, a design process runs the risk of producing form devoid of the intentionality of an integrated design.

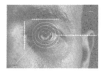    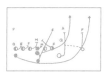 

Pattern recognition in artificial and natural intelligence

Following the idea of intelligence is design invention. Integrated, built upon previous innovation, and driven toward a reconfiguration of the known or accepted, invention is like the patent office of possible design approaches; it is the repository of potentials from which we draw to produce alternative readings or formulations. Invention, for us, is embedded in architecture and urban design that rethink organizational systems, spatial and formal configurations, type, technology, and constructed and natural systems. These sorts of projects that invent, delight, and perhaps confound do so in various ways. Seemingly irrational programmatic laminations can produce a new rationality that reorients preconceived ideas of function and adjacency. Innovation in structure and materiality can change ideas of possible or accepted forms and dimensions of buildings.

The work that we include in this book is presented in written, drawn, modeled, and built form. The projects range from the theoretical and speculative to the built, but building and the way things are put together is central to all the works. We test our beliefs as architects through the logics of built form. Issues of efficiency, technology, and constructability are integral to our design process, not externally applied upon later assessment. For us, a pattern-recognition scheme is incomplete without the material, physical, and phenomenological concerns that built form requires. And the work that we produce is an amalgam of the forces—both determined and imposed—and elements—both stable and unstable—in an architectural agglomeration. In this regard, the ultimate goal of pattern recognition, as we define it, is not mere pattern, but more building.

## Pattern Recognition in Artificial Intelligence

In artificial-intelligence parlance, pattern recognition defines methodologies for the classification of information "observed" by machines. These machines use previously described or statistically derived patterns to make voice, face, and hand identifications, as well as text and graphic determinations, and the patterns they use conform to one of three basic categorical methodologies: syntactic, statistical, and neural.

A syntactic classification scheme operates on the structural interrelationships among elements; a statistical classification scheme analyzes data, statistics, and numerical information in order to group and identify similarities and traits; a neural classification scheme is an adaptive, network-based analysis that identifies organizational systems by means of nonlinear statistical data–modeling methodologies.

The applications of these AI processes mainly appear in the programming of computers, directing the computers to do what human beings (and bees and starlings) innately do: extract organizations of constituent components that define points in particular multidimensional spaces. No surprise, then, that the term carries a fascination and an eerie sci-fi connotation, since humans are transferring identification and decision-making functions over to machines. Witness the burgeoning field of biometrics, in which machines are programmed to make real-time identifications of people by using differences as points of reference in a field of likeness. And, similarly, in architecture, where the use of computer scripting through data input and algorithmic procedures generates forms that are considered to be products of their data. Suffice it to say that we reject this school of thought for our practice and process, because it gives away the agency of the architect to artificially cognizant but nonsentient machines. For us, pattern recognition, in its observations, diagramming, and focus on construction methods, necessitates the architect as the driver of intentionality and, ultimately, form.

In our work, we transform these three basic AI organizational constructs (syntactic, statistical, and neural) into dynamic and nonlinear methodologies. In this way, pattern recognition functions more as a filter for understanding and navigating a problem—as the means of a design (process), not the end (product).

## Pattern Recognition in Natural Intelligence

Visual arts, scholastic and optics testing, the ability of birds to flock and of bees to recognize hive mates and human faces, are all non-AI examples of pattern recognition. The diversity of users of this process of classifying and acting on observations of patterns attests to the fundamental nature of pattern recognition as a navigational and survival trait in human and animal cognition. Pattern, as any traffic engineer will tell you, is about flows, bottlenecks, detours, and schedules. It is also about crime solving, weather modeling, finding cures for diseases, and making financial determinations. In William Gibson's novel *Pattern Recognition*,[1] the ability to see and interpret patterns is fundamental to survival in global subcultures of underground Internet video trading and "cool hunting" (a rarified art form whose high period peaked in the dot-com era but is still actively practiced in the determination of global and regional street style and, indeed, architectural style). In Gibson's reading, pattern recognition is both "a gift and a trap" in that it facilitates a close reading of traits and trends, but it runs the risk of overgeneralization.[2]

For us, pattern recognition is incomplete if pure categorization or identification is the end in itself. As architects employing a process-based approach to the search for form— or what we call the "informal formal"—we run our observations through a filter of intention-laden analysis and diagramming in order to produce architectural solutions. This intentionality, in contrast to the unintentional architecture designed by machines, is a critical part of our definition of this process, since it encompasses everything that we bring to bear on our practice. Our approach utilizes artificial and natural methodologies of pattern recognition, as well as popular cultural engagements and architectural history and theory, as instruments for understanding generalized similarities and for producing difference from specificities. It also seeks out variations in scale within the diagrams we produce in order to determine building and material logics in a design scheme.

## Syntactic, Statistical, and Neural Organizations

Using the same terms of AI pattern recognition, we employ the three methodologies—syntactic, statistical, and neural— as the basis for understanding architectural organizational strategies, and looking beyond to further design potentials. A syntactic scheme operates on the structural interrelationships among physical elements and points toward built and natural morphologies. A statistical scheme analyzes data, statistics, and information and, by extension, relates to a program- and inventory-focused project organization. And a neural scheme is a network-intensive analysis, emphasizing circulation, infrastructure, and social and temporal impacts on a building or city. Within a given project, these three pattern methods apply to various components of the architecture, most often with one predominating and acting as the driving methodology. However, so as not to misrepresent this process as overly deterministic of pure classification, we should emphasize our perception of these organization and classification strategies as open categories that cross over one another among and within projects and apply variably across building and design systems. We understand the road, as part of a larger transportation network, to be a predominantly neural construct, for example; but we also see the statistical elements (the parcel structure and associated dimensions of the lots and buildings fronting the road) it comprises and the syntactic characteristics (the curvature of the road in relation to the topographical forms) that influence it. These terms are further explained below in brief descriptions of specific projects.

Structure, natural and built form, and the interrelationships among material components are foregrounded in syntactically organized projects. Mixed Greens, a gallery project in New York City, deploys its forms, materials, and infrastructures around an existing structural beam-and-column configuration.

All aspects of the project—light, air, circulation, sprinklers— coalesce at the ceiling design, the collector of all design and infrastructural elements. CC01 House, located in rural New York State, is composed of a linear organization of sliding volumes that emerged from an analysis of the long thin lines of crops that had been farmed on the land for many years. The forms, systems, infrastructures, and materials are configured to extend and exploit this linear configuration. Spaces Between the Hills, an urban project for the city of Jerusalem, responds to the natural valley systems that divide communities and proposes to connect the ideologically divided neighborhoods with bridge structures that contain shared programs, circulation, and all manner of infrastructure for the sustenance of the two adjacent communities. Wetland City, another urban design project, located in the flood-damaged area of New Orleans East, takes on the rising Louisiana and Gulf Coast water levels and wetland destruction. In this design for a city of a hundred thousand people, housing, parks, transit stations, and civic and institutional buildings are built on new and reclaimed elevated structural and infrastructural grounds that are protected by reinforced wetlands. This project proposes what we call an "integrated aqua-urbanism" through the construction of elevated flood-safe neighborhoods and reinforced natural systems.

Programmatic components, the inventory of elements, and numerically derived organizations drive statistical projects. We transform the data or inventory of a problem into an organizational scheme based on cataloging and indexical systems. (This information, in contrast to recent data-mapping endeavors in architecture, is local—specific to the precise stuff of a project—not a grafting of material external to the parameters of a project.) An example of a statistical project is VVE House, a renovation of a garage building in rural upstate New York, which takes its cue from the settlement patterns of drifting farm and residential buildings along a road. Each building in this organization is defined by its function (house, barn, garage) and has a distinct relationship to the road. This pattern of individually drifting buildings is then utilized to formulate a similar drift pattern of discrete programmatic boxes of dwelling components (bathroom, kitchen, storage space, equipment room). Chicago Filter Park, a project for a thousand-car parking facility, is a statistically driven project in that the constantly changing schedule of the garage and the automated mechanism that moves the cars are made visible from the highway by the glass facade that covers the long, thin building. The facade is thus a sign composed of the inventory of parked cars in the garage, revealing how full or empty the garage is throughout the day. Two exhibitions of our work, in New York and Texas, are inventory-based projects. In these installations, the components and dimensions of the material used for display correlate to the number and square footage of the projects exhibited.

In neural organizational schemes, the architecture is driven by circulation, infrastructure, and social and temporal patterns. Projects that follow a neural methodology are largely network-based and foreground circulation and movement, as well as

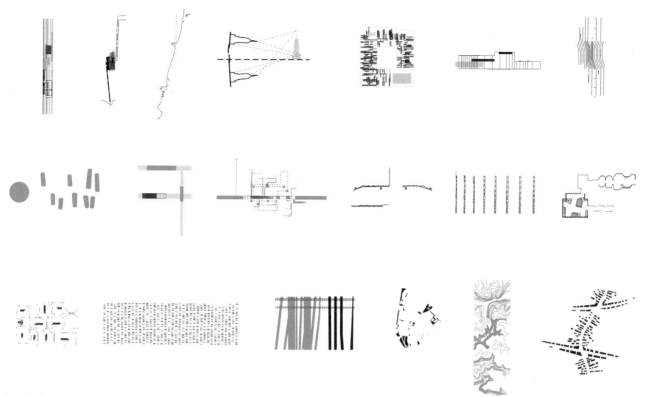

Local codes: project diagrams

mechanical, plumbing, and electrical systems. EMR Printing Plant centrally positions a circulation space that feeds all programs, processes, and movement into a long double-height volume. This central volume, which contains all aspects of the movement and infrastructure of the facility, is essentially the motherboard of a circuit diagram to which all equipment and programs are connected. Nassau Street Lobby, a project for a residential apartment building, is based on patterns of movement and activity. The temporal patterns of tenants and visitors are tracked and calibrated in the material surfaces and joint patterns. The resultant patterns of the architecture encode movement patterns and sequences of activity in the lobby. Finally, Cedarhurst Spiral Housing, a scheme for an apartment building in a predominantly orthodox Jewish community, is organized around an array of circulation and infrastructure. In this example, the architecture embeds the spiral of vehicular and pedestrian movement in the building's organization, infrastructure, and green, public, and private spaces.

## Local Code

In architecture and urban design, codes are sets of rules that dictate form and construction practices. Building codes run the gamut from national to local laws. Codes in localities prescribe relationships between buildings, streets, and natural systems; building heights; how utilities serve buildings; construction classifications, construction systems, and types of equipment that can be used in buildings. Charged largely with public safety, building codes and especially zoning codes often create numbing generalization and uniformity. In pattern recognition, a code has a very different definition for us and serves a different function. In this sense, a code, a local code of a project, is the particular focus of that project, whether site-, program-, or system-driven. Our local code is further differentiated from a building code in that it emerges from a process that determines the specific qualities of a project. This process prioritizes difference above homogenization through the deep analytical study engaged by the pattern-recognition process.

Within any of the above-mentioned organizational schemes, which address assemblies, inventories, and flows, we seek the particular, as opposed to the general, in the selected pattern. Our pattern-recognition methodologies also differ in this way from AI processes that are directed toward identification, or a machinic endgame. To get at this specific coding of a project, we graph, group, draw lines between things, laminate, trace, and separate out elements to see what they mean, what they look like, and what they suggest. And as an investigation is embedded with internal conditions of site, program, technology, etc., there is a distinct locality to the process. As a result, these elements contain various grains, from coarse to fine, of a project's concepts and parameters. To determine this local code, we produce a myriad of diagrams during the course of a project and distill it into generative code, against which the work can be evaluated during the design process. This local

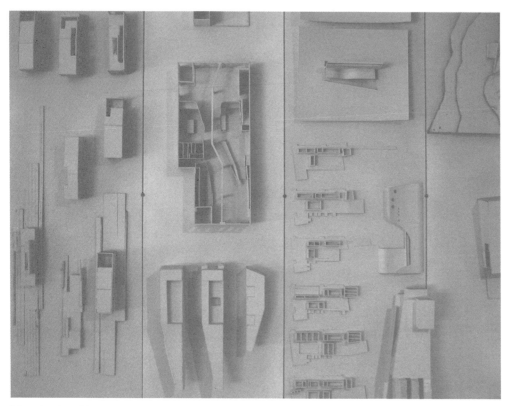

Informal study models

code is essentially a drawing or diagram that embeds a concept.

City of Stockholm Public Library Addition is a project that displays this idea of local code at various levels of solid and void: the water-to-land relationship of the region; the archi-tectural morphology of the city blocks, built fully around the perimeter with courtyards in the middle; and the original Asplund Library, with the central rotunda as an empty space. Using this solid/void local code, we embed a series of infra-structural skylights (voids) within each of the departments added to the existing library. These voids are a series of illuminated yellow holes around which people and books collect. In another example, Chelsea Penthouse, the local code is driven by the project's proximity to the skyline view of the Empire State Building and a desire to bring the view into the space of the apartment. The resultant design consists of the conver-gence of two angled glass planes that capture and double the particular view. And, lastly, Les Migrateurs Furniture Showroom has a local code that arranges, within a three-dimensional grid, alternative ways of viewing displayed objects, from below and above, through holes in the floor and ceiling.

## Informal Formal

Seemingly paradoxical, "informal formal" describes an oscilla-tion in our form-making process between a project's local code as it exists in diagrammatic form and the necessity to formulate that code into a building, replete with systems, materials, and details. Informal formal approximates the conceptual world of theoretical constructs and diagrams into the real world of materials and built form, where the rubber of pattern recog-nition hits the road. Illustrative here is the logical "theory of fuzziness" that confronts real-world applications and celebrates the imperfection of a rigid classification system in order to address complex problems.[3] This idea of fuzziness illuminates our definition of the informal formal.

The informal is a free-form state of open possibilities. It promotes a permissive sampling of potentials and allows us to graze, especially at the beginning of a project while learning the conditions of the problem. Moreover, informality allows for a questioning of conventions as they relate to the way buildings should look and materials should be used.

If the informal allows for casualness and seeming instabil-ity, stability and rigor inheres in the formal. Formal also carries with it the idea of form—form as the result of a process and form as a container of the intentions of the project. And, for us, form is required for pattern-recognition to be understood as a transformative process that produces architecture through diagramming. Form is the embodiment of what we study and care about, because it is the final conveyor of architectural intentions. We seek the informality of an idea, a material, or a system in its raw state and the formality of precision required to make this condition legible.

Within our interpretations of syntactic, statistical, and neural organizations, informal formal—which is our brand of fuzziness—addresses the actual stuff of building, the material elements, the ultimate constraints of a pattern-recognition process. It follows that the transformation from an idea into a building is not a seamless process; it necessarily involves approximation and a determined push toward design.

## Material Methodologies

Material considerations embody the tropes to which an architecture practice returns and on which it expands throughout from project to project. Certain architecture practices utilize the same materials over and over, developing a material style as a result. Others make sure to use new and different materials in nearly every project. In our work, material methodologies emerge from the informal formal process, by which the singular material or combination of materials throws the idea of the building into high relief. As a result, we may at times have a reductive palette of materials and colors, but they always address the particularities of a project, a process, or a client's desires. Below we describe various material approaches and physical characteristics in our work. They carry weight, dimension, monetary value, and degrees of efficiency. We also include perceptual techniques, since they engage the physicality of the idea in the same way that materials do in an architectural scheme. We are all too aware that this approach runs the risk of a stylistic materiality within which the work can get stuck. However, since our work is based in pattern recognition as a process, we believe that these material concerns approach locality as opposed to stylistic proclivity.

Green and its attendant contested term *sustainability* are embedded in our work. Orientation to the sun, appropriate technologies, nontoxic materials, and natural ventilation take precedence over a LEED checklist of a prescribed set of rules. These concerns are added into the mix of possible design generators so as not to be tacked on after the fact. Green as a material—trees and plantings—also occupies an integral and pragmatic part of our architecture. Trees and plantings find their own zone, strip, field, or vector in a design diagram and, when built/planted, enhance the health of the buildings. Chicago Filter Park, Greenwich Street Park Apartments, and the Filter Parking project in general all exemplify the use of green as an air-quality experience and aesthetic methodology. In Chicago Filter Park, trees hang at the crossing points of lateral bracing components and tall grasses cover portions of the rooftop park and cafe, the highway-spanning meadow, and the air-filtering berms at street level.

Structure is an elemental aspect of a building scheme. The physicality of structure is undeniable, whether exposed or just made necessary for a design to succeed. The structural system of a project may be more visible if it is driving the idea, or it might recede if it is a secondary idea. This material methodology is a primary instrument in the Catskills House, where the forms of the building slip past one another to create a shift that reinforces the stepping diagram of the project. This slip of one volume off the other requires a cantilever at the end of the building to make the idea of shift legible. The structural condition is in this case perceptible; but the steel required for the cantilever was not exposed, so that the form of the building

Material methodologies: detail at Nassau Street lobby

would be emphasized, not the structural maneuvering. Chicago Filter Park relies on the exposed structural steel grid and cross-bracing to achieve its lightness and transparency—something not usually seen in a parking garage. The lightness of the steel structure is central to the idea of the garage and therefore more visible and present. In the urban proposal for the city of Jerusalem, Spaces Between the Hills, the technology of highway-bridge structures creates spans that join disparate neighborhoods. These valley-crossing structures drove the design of each of the three projects.

Infrastructure is inherent to a neural system and is networked and circulatory by nature. Infrastructure is foregrounded in many of our projects. Mixed Greens, a project for an art gallery, has its wiggling ceiling that contains all necessary mechanical components of air, light, and sprinklers. EMR Printing Plant is a circuit diagram for people and equipment in a production sequence. Chicago Filter Park is an urban pedestrian-and-cyclist bridge that bundles public and private transportation with public-park programs. Spaces Between the Hills proposes infrastructural bridges for the region surrounding Jerusalem. And Wetland City, in New Orleans East, is a linear network of public infrastructure and neighborhoods.

Surface is but one property of any material, but it carries with it texture and pattern that one can immediately see and touch. The Catskills House celebrates surface through the specific properties of the exterior cladding material. The cedar siding at the upper level uses the dimension of standard lengths of horizontal board, along with areas of overlap, to modulate pattern and create a linear, textured wall surface. The bottom volume of the house, clad in light-gray fiber-cement board, shifts the four-foot-by-ten-foot panels vertically off one another to address the dimension of the material in relation to the height of the wall. This surface—chalky to the touch—is a much more uniform treatment than the wood above.

Views are perceptual and experiential and therefore physically embedded in a building scheme by configurations that frame views through the strategic placement of windows. CC01 House employs a series of specific small-framed views played off against big open views afforded by entire walls of glass. Nassau Street Lobby frames reflected interior views of the outdoor and indoor space. Similarly, Les Migrateurs Furniture Showroom frames views of furniture by means of cuts in the floor and ceiling of the two-story space. And VVE House utilizes outward views toward the landscape and surrounding buildings and interrelates those views with specific programmatic components of the house.

Light and luminosity are, for us, instruments for revealing or slightly concealing significant spatial and material conditions. Light can convey the intention of a space, dematerialize it, or it can be physical in its materiality by means of surfaces that glow. Several of our furniture projects employ a glowing surface, either through integrated artificial light or through the use of thick frosted acrylic, resins, or other light-transmitting materials. Stockholm Library Addition is organized around yellow-glass light voids that illuminate the library departments throughout the year with both natural and artificial light. EMR Printing Plant employs an eighty-foot-long translucent volume, with light inside, that glows deep into the floor plate of the building. CC01 House plays its flat, black exterior against a luminous, white interior. The ceiling of Mixed Greens Gallery is essentially a light box—a light fixture with smaller lights shooting out of its defined volume. And the two exhibitions of our work, LB Exhibitions, both use fluorescent lights and translucent Mylar to form lines of light into an installation of glowing strips of displayed projects.

Color (or, in many cases, the absence of color) is an important consideration in our work. Black-White-Gray-Glow, muted and absent of color, is employed in many of our projects. This palette of "non-color" at once emphasizes the architectural space with the natural play of light and shadow and celebrates the non-architectural context of a project. When we do employ color, it carries a specific agenda to call out difference and significance. The gallery project, Mixed Greens—mostly white, gray (aluminum), and glow—uses color to distinguish inside from outside, private from public, non–art wall from art wall. Taking the obvious cue from the gallery name, different shades of green are applied to the interiors of the office and storage spaces, bathrooms, and the insides of closets and cabinetry. CC01 House is black, white, and gray (aluminum) but frames the colors of the seasons through the windows. Stockholm Library Addition is primarily gray (metal), clear (glass), and white (interiors) but explodes with yellow light at the nine skylight voids. VVE House wraps a light-gray metal exterior around a white interior, in which individual black wood boxes contain an earthy yellow palette on their interior surface volumes.

Assembly and detail are the methods that coalesce all of our organizational systems: they're how it all comes together. Nassau Street Lobby uses exposed stainless-steel brackets, thumbscrews, and surgical tubing to reveal the tenuous nature of hanging large pieces of glass off a wall, while CC01 House uses detail not only to keep water out of the building, but also

to create taut transitions from one material to the next. Mixed Greens Gallery utilizes strategies similar to those of both of the above-mentioned projects, with an emphasis on detailing the ceiling so that the diagram is easily read in the built product. And LB Exhibitions addresses the challenge of low budget and quick assembly by using standard aluminum framing members as display devices and simple fluorescent lights for the illumination of the interior volume—creating linear light boxes for display.

### Reflexive Pattern Recognition
This book describes the working methodology that we have devised in the first ten years of our practice, from 1997 to 2007. We acknowledge that encapsulating a body of work in a single monograph suggests a continuity that is oftentimes artificial. However, we have found that it does, in fact, reveal underlying operative methodologies in our practice. The book, then, has been a reflexive pattern-recognition process that has brought to light how we work and how we want to proceed in the future of our practice. In this regard, this book, while a summary of the first phase of our practice, is perhaps more of a preface to the next.

———
1. William Gibson, *Pattern Recognition* (New York: The Berkley Publishing Group, 2003).
2. William Gibson, *Pattern Recognition*, 22.
3. James Bezdek, et al., *Fuzzy Models and Algorithms for Pattern Recognition and Image Processing* (New York: Springer Science + Business Media, Inc, 2005).

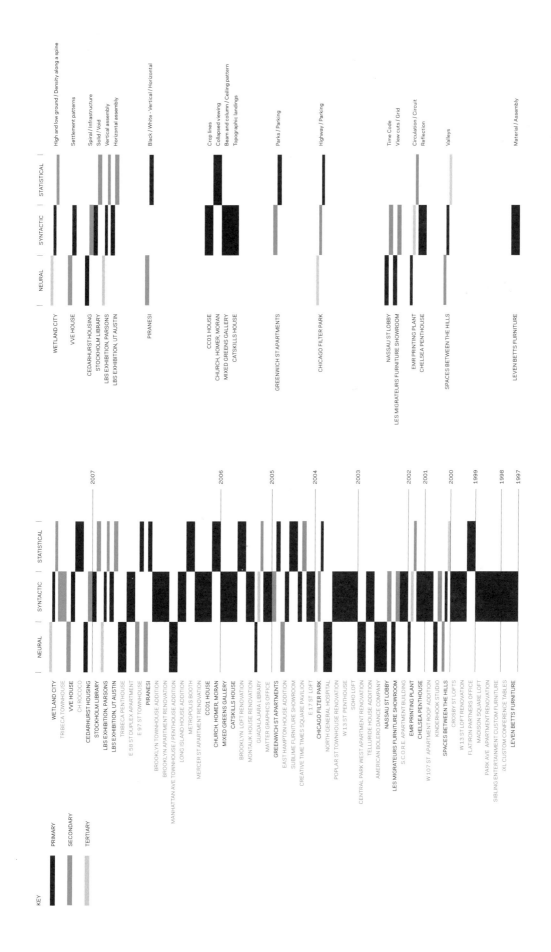

Methodology Chart

Reflexive pattern recognition: organizational methodologies of projects

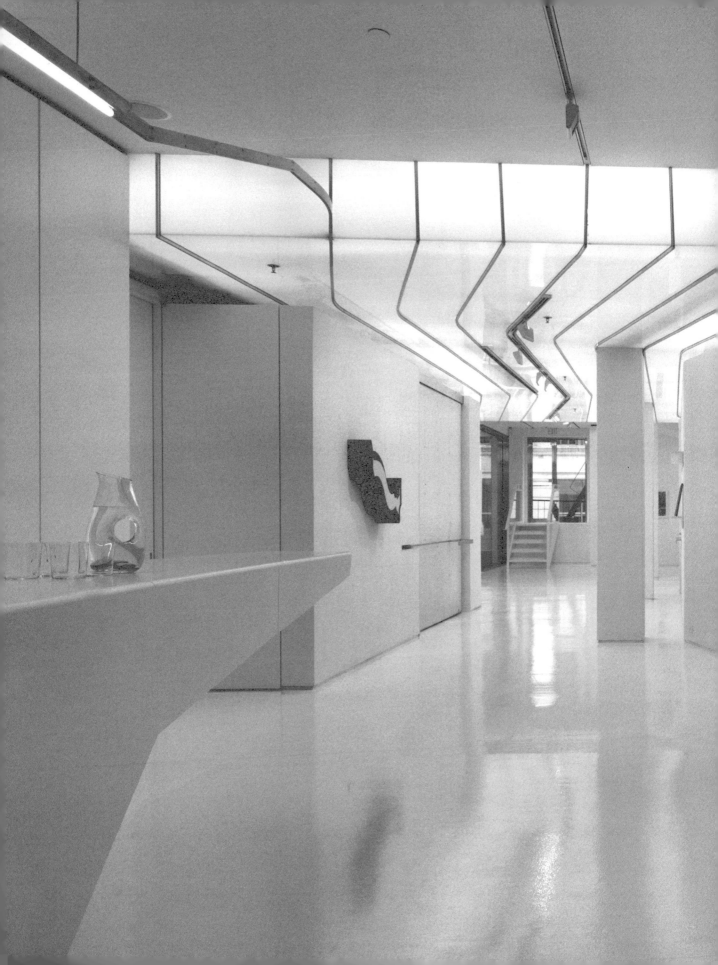

# CC01 House

LOCATION: COLUMBIA COUNTY, NEW YORK / PROGRAM: RESIDENTIAL
ORGANIZATION: SYNTACTIC / LOCAL CODE: CROP LINES
AREA: 2,000 SF / COMPLETION DATE: 2006

The design of the CC01 House begins with a reading of the landscape. Long linear grooves, formed by the dimensions of machinery, the distance between tractor wheels, and the frequency of the blades of a plow, are etched into the rolling hills from years of farming. These lines that hug the topography were developed into diagrams that inform the design of all configurations of the house, from the primary organization and form to the cladding and details of the building. Additionally, the section of the house follows the contour of the land as it steps up from east to west in the long outdoor terrace and again between the dining and living spaces of the house. In this way, the house follows the landscape and topography both in plan and in section.

The programmatic spaces of the house are divided between two linear volumes, one wet and the other dry. The wet zone—consisting of bathrooms, kitchen, laundry, and utilities—occupies a long, thin volume, whereas the dry zone—consisting of the living and dining rooms and bedrooms—exists in a wider volume that provides for more generous spaces. Set into the thinner volume (the wet zone), the infrastructure of water, waste, and gas piping and heat production and dis-tribution is an attenuated network of piping and valves. These systems, particularly the plumbing, begin at the well outside the house, run in a line into the long, thin basement, continue through the house, and then exit into the septic tank and leach field, all along lines of the diagram. The two volumes slide past each other as they follow the linear farming pattern. Inside, the twenty-foot-long kitchen counter overlaps the two volumes at the ground floor, drawing together the working (wet) and living (dry) spaces.

Several other elements follow the linear crop diagram, such as the horizontally oriented corrugated-metal siding; patio paving patterns; plantings around the house; the punched windows on the long elevations and adjacent horizontal streaks of flat panels; and the attenuated retaining walls, which are extensions of the long walls of the foundation. These retaining walls extend into the landscape, inscribe the land, and define the exterior spaces of the garage, entry walkway, and two patios. The linear configuration is further emphasized by the tubular form of the house's two volumes, which are mostly open on their short ends but are more solid on the long faces. Composed primarily of large glass windows and sliding doors, the short elevations frame views of the cultivated fields on one end and of the neighboring farmer's compound on the other.

Northwest view

The long elevations contain smaller horizontal windows, which isolate specific scenes around the house. The structure of the house conforms to this open-versus-solid condition of the walls in that the long walls (and most of the house) are wood-framed, while the short end walls use steel moment frames to allow for total glass infill at these locations.

The upper floor of the house comprises two large bedrooms, with corresponding bathrooms, and an open study in between. Below, the living areas of the house flow into one another and are bounded by views of fields on one side and a long outdoor terrace on the other. This east-facing terrace near the dining area is the primary outdoor space of the house and is dominated by a sixteen-foot-long concrete counter with a built-in gas barbecue and firewood storage below. From the counter, which also doubles as an outdoor dining table, one can enjoy far-reaching views of the distant mountain range and changing weather conditions. At the end of the terrace is a translucent garage, clad entirely in polycarbonate, whose interior lighting allows it to glow at night like a lantern. The secondary outdoor space is a smaller terrace located at the west end of the house, on the side opposite the long terrace. It faces northwest and captures summer sunset views. Both terraces result from the two volumes of the house shifting off each other in plan.

The kitchen, located in the overlap between the wet and dry zones of the house, is a floating white linear box. At its supported end, the counter sits at the top of a series of concrete steps, while at the floating end, it juts out from a cantilevered steel carriage that is supported by the main column of the house. This twenty-foot-long counter contains the cooktop, sink, and two dishwashers, as well as storage.

The refrigerator, oven, and pantry are all located in the cabinetry behind the floating counter.

The color palette of the house, Black-White-Gray-Glow, is derived from five basic materials: black metal siding, white interior walls and cabinets, gray metal and concrete, and glowing plastic. The black aluminum siding of the exterior, with horizontally oriented corrugations, attenuates the form of the house and contrasts starkly with the white surfaces of the interior. Gray, used as a mediator between black and white, occurs at all metalwork; and, in the case of the windows and doors, it is the color of the raw aluminum. The stair is made of eight-inch steel channels with bolted diamond plate treads. The rail of the stair and the opening at the study is welded steel flat bar with socket-head screws tapped into the bar with polyester sleeves as glazing stops. The master bedroom sink base is made of welded mill-finish aluminum flat bar with stainless-steel mechanical fasteners. Glow is achieved by using translucent polycarbonate to cover large window openings, providing privacy and diffuse light. As mentioned above, the garage is clad entirely in this material, creating glow but also contrasting with the house's black exterior and the landscape. Depending on the season, this neutral palette either creates a stark contrast between the house and the outdoor landscape or blurs the distinction. In the snow, when viewed from the outside, the all-black exterior stands out sharply against the white fields; but from the inside, the white interiors and glowing surfaces blend into the white landscape. And during the spring, summer, and fall, the vibrant outdoor colors are framed in the windows against the white-and-gray interior. In this way, the interior of the house becomes a mute frame for views onto the landscape.

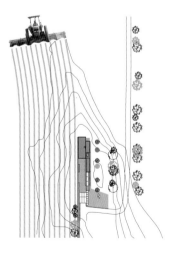

left: Crop lines as site patterns
right: Site plan with tractor

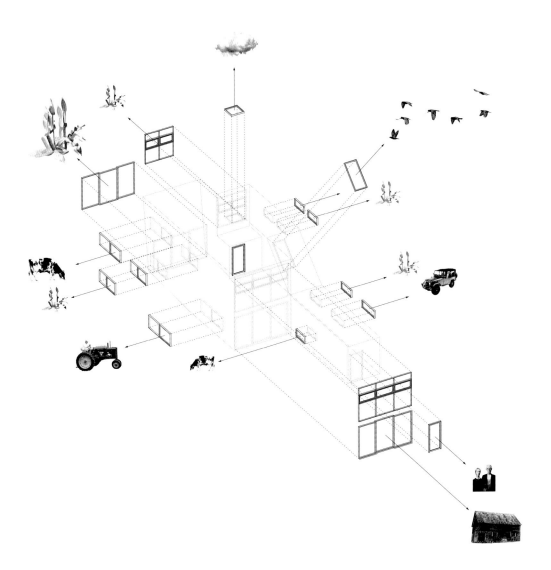

top: Exploded diagram of views and window types
bottom, left to right: Southwest view, Southeast view, View from patio

1  Garage
2  Entry ramp
3  Patio
4  Barbecue
5  Entry
6  Closet
7  Bathroom
8  Kitchen
9  Dining room
10 Living room
11 Bedroom
12 Study

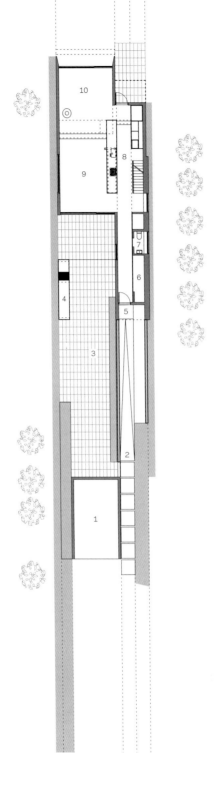

First-floor plan ⌐——————⌐ 15' ◔          Second-floor plan

top left: Northeast view
top right: West view
bottom: Southeast view at dusk

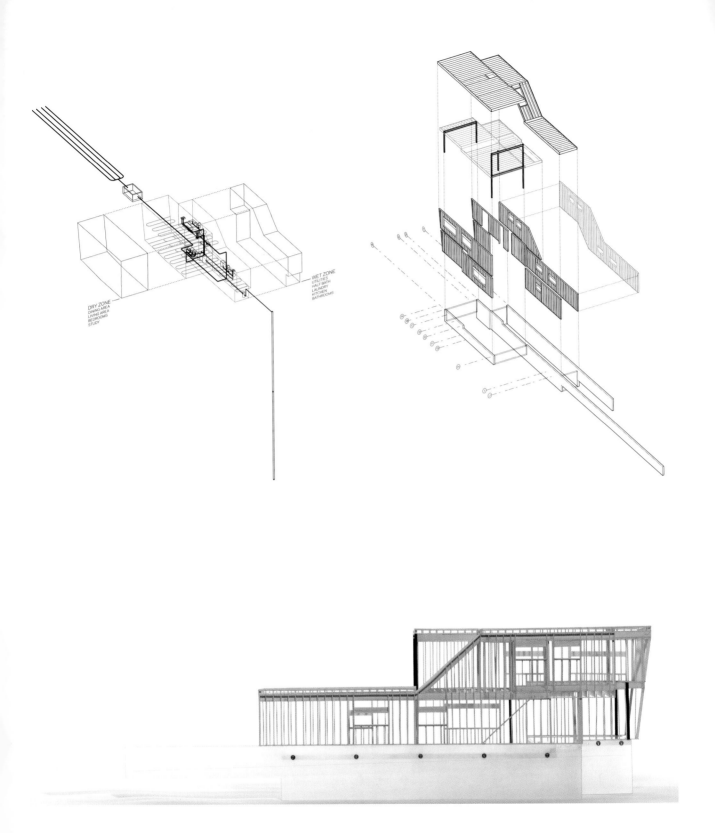

DRY ZONE
DINING AREA
LIVING AREA
BEDROOMS
STUDY

WET ZONE
UTILITIES
HALF BATH
LAUNDRY
KITCHEN
BATHROOMS

**top left:** Wet zone versus dry zone: all plumbing functions and fixtures are in the long thin bar; all living programs are in the short wide bar
**top right:** Foundation and framing: long walls are wood framed; short end walls are spanned by steel moment frames and left open for glass
**bottom:** Framing model

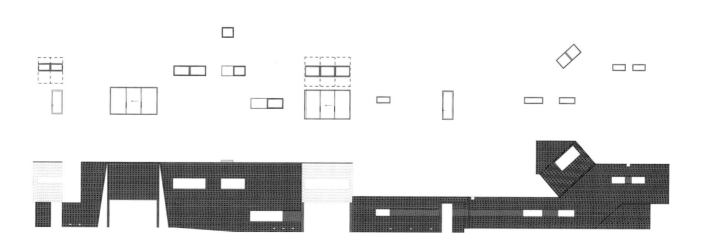

**top left:** North wall window and siding detail
**top right:** Northwest view
**bottom:** Unfolded siding and window elevations

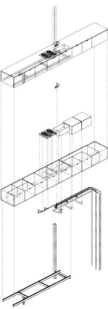

**opposite:** View through house from west
**top:** View from living area to kitchen and dining
**bottom left:** View from entry hall
**bottom right:** Exploded kitchen plumbing and cabinetry

**left:** Second-floor entry to bedroom under skylight
**right:** Second-floor study

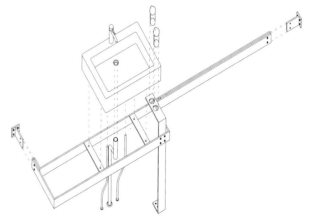

top: Bedroom and bathroom
bottom: Sink carriage axonometric: demountable aluminum flat bar
with stainless steel fasteners

# Catskills House

LOCATION: STONE RIDGE, NEW YORK / PROGRAM: RESIDENTIAL
ORGANIZATION: SYNTACTICAL / LOCAL CODE: STEPPED LANDSCAPE
AREA: 2,400 SF / COMPLETION DATE: 2005

The site of this house is a wooded eleven-acre parcel of land that is distinguished by a slope that begins gently, drops off precipitously, and then flattens out at a wide stream that runs the full width of the property. The house sits at the crest of the ridge and addresses the topography by stepping down toward the water. A series of natural landings enables passage down the steep ridge toward the stream. These landings serve as the primary generator of the design of the house.

Each landing is spaced and dimensioned in response to the movement of an individual's negotiation of the slope. There are faster steps approaching the house; slower steps at the ridge, middle, and entry areas of the house; and then quicker steps again as one descends the flatter topography toward the stream.

The landscape, the view of the water to the east, and the orientation of the site toward the sun are the primary physical characteristics addressed by the house. Mostly open, with glass at the ground floor, the first level of the house is conceived as one of the landings in the landscape, as is the second level, which is lifted above the platform system and more enclosed. This upper level functions as a refuge in the trees where the land falls away.

The stepping of the house is achieved by sliding the upper volume of the house off the lower volume. This shift creates two exterior spaces: the covered parking area at the first floor and the master-bedroom deck at the second floor. The lower step is supported from the foundation wall below, whereas the upper step, with its cantilevered end, requires structural steel in order to make the back end float above the parking area with only two support columns below.

The exterior cladding of the house expresses this shift between levels by using two distinct materials above and below. The upper level is clad in horizontal shiplap cedar siding boards that are four inches in width. The length of each board is selected and coordinated so that the pattern of joints creates a subtle rhythm of vertical lines that correlates to the openings and cabinetry inside the house. Conversely, the lower level is clad in vertically oriented light-gray cement-board panels that are eight feet high by four feet wide. The overall height of the lower level's exterior wall is twelve feet, so the siding pattern is created by shifting panels.

Furthering the reading of one volume shifting off the other to make a step, the upper cedar siding sits outboard of the cement-board siding, making the house look at its east end as though it has slid open and pulled away from the lower level.

The roof of the house reverses the typical slope configuration. The planes of the roof slope inward to a scupper on the north side of the house, and as a result, three sides of the house appear to have a flat roof. This inverted-roof geometry created by the sloping configuration is visible as a folded plane from the interior of the house at the second floor.

Inside, a linear organization of storage boxes runs lengthwise through the house on both floors. At the first floor, the storage boxes separate the entry from the dining and kitchen areas. On the second floor, the storage boxes separate the hallway from the bedrooms. Access to the cabinets occurs on both sides, depending on use. This storage volume, at both levels of the house, is also the infrastructural zone, containing areas for laundry, ductwork, and plumbing. The storage cabinetry is made of vertical-grain Douglas fir both upstairs and downstairs, so that the reading of the volumes is consistent throughout the house.

The interior of the house is organized by prioritizing views out on the trees and the stream. Beginning at the entry and continuing through each room, the focal point is always oriented outward. As one enters a space, a window or door is placed on axis, framing a broad view of the landscape or a single tree.

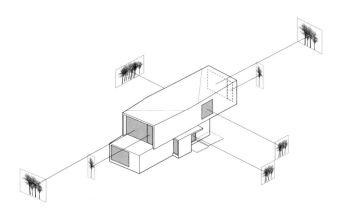

right: View diagram
opposite: View at entry with stepped landings

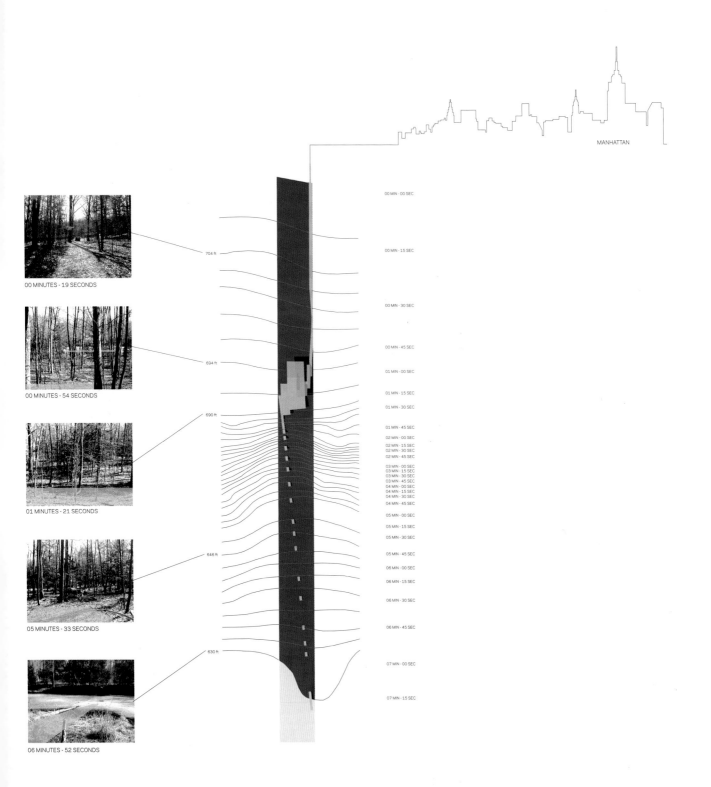

MANHATTAN

00 MINUTES - 19 SECONDS

00 MINUTES - 54 SECONDS

01 MINUTES - 21 SECONDS

05 MINUTES - 33 SECONDS

06 MINUTES - 52 SECONDS

704 ft

694 ft

690 ft

646 ft

630 ft

00 MIN - 00 SEC

00 MIN - 15 SEC

00 MIN - 30 SEC

00 MIN - 45 SEC

01 MIN - 00 SEC

01 MIN - 15 SEC

01 MIN - 30 SEC

01 MIN - 45 SEC
02 MIN - 00 SEC
02 MIN - 15 SEC
02 MIN - 30 SEC
02 MIN - 45 SEC

03 MIN - 00 SEC
03 MIN - 15 SEC
03 MIN - 30 SEC
03 MIN - 45 SEC
04 MIN - 00 SEC
04 MIN - 15 SEC
04 MIN - 30 SEC
04 MIN - 45 SEC

05 MIN - 00 SEC

05 MIN - 15 SEC

05 MIN - 30 SEC

05 MIN - 45 SEC

06 MIN - 00 SEC

06 MIN - 15 SEC

06 MIN - 30 SEC

06 MIN - 45 SEC

07 MIN - 00 SEC

07 MIN - 15 SEC

Temporal diagram of movement pattern through the site

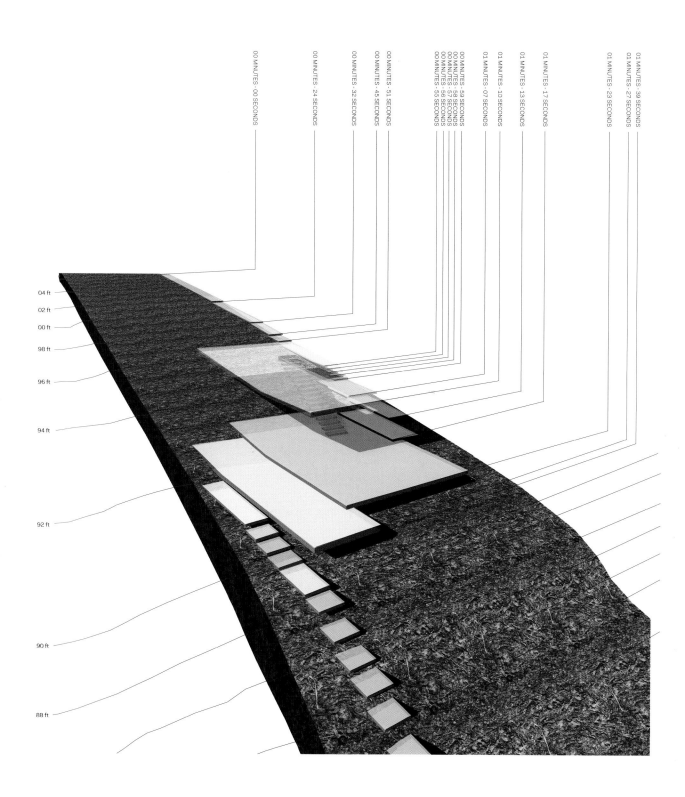

04 ft
02 ft
00 ft
98 ft
96 ft
94 ft
92 ft
90 ft
88 ft

00 MINUTES · 00 SECONDS
00 MINUTES · 24 SECONDS
00 MINUTES · 32 SECONDS
00 MINUTES · 45 SECONDS
00 MINUTES · 51 SECONDS
00 MINUTES · 55 SECONDS
00 MINUTES · 56 SECONDS
00 MINUTES · 57 SECONDS
00 MINUTES · 58 SECONDS
00 MINUTES · 59 SECONDS
01 MINUTES · 07 SECONDS
01 MINUTES · 10 SECONDS
01 MINUTES · 13 SECONDS
01 MINUTES · 17 SECONDS
01 MINUTES · 23 SECONDS
01 MINUTES · 27 SECONDS
01 MINUTES · 39 SECONDS

Site landings and speed-of-movement study

1   Parking
2   Entry
3   Living/dining area
4   Kitchen
5   WC
6   Storage
7   Mechanical
8   Study
9   Bedroom
10  Bathroom
11  Deck

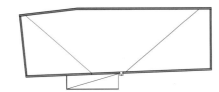

Roof plan

Second-floor plan

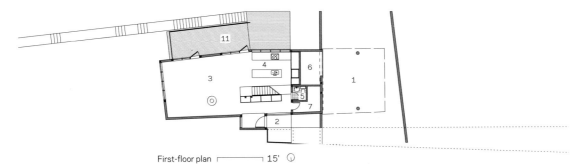

First-floor plan ⌐━━━━━┐ 15' ⊕

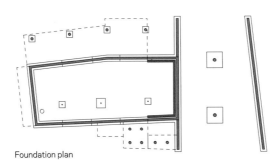

Foundation plan

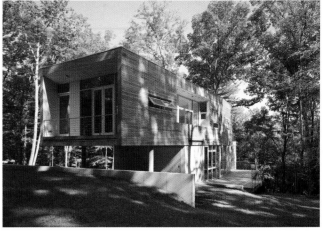

top left: North view
top right: Southwest view
bottom: South view

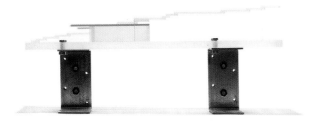

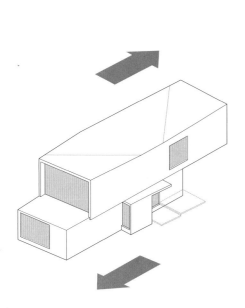

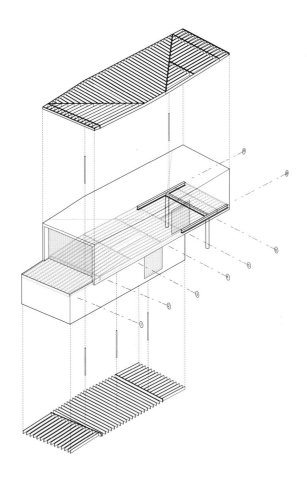

**top:** Study model of landings
**bottom left:** Shift diagram
**bottom right:** Exploded framing isometric: steel cantilever
affords the shift of volumes

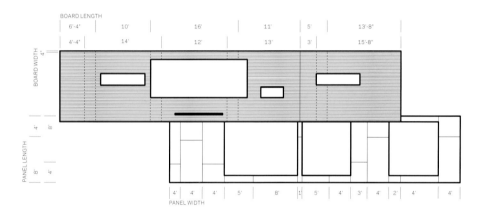

BOARD LENGTH
6'-4" | 10' | 16' | 11' | 5' | 13'-8"
4'-4" | 14' | 12' | 13' | 3' | 15'-8"

BOARD WIDTH: 4"

PANEL LENGTH: 4' | 8' | 8' | 4'

PANEL WIDTH: 4' | 4' | 4' | 5' | 8' | 1' | 5' | 4' | 3' | 4' | 2' | 4' | 4'

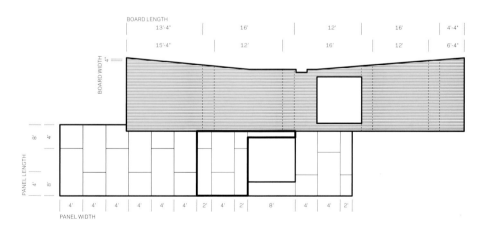

BOARD LENGTH
13'-4" | 16' | 12' | 16' | 4'-4"
15'-4" | 12' | 16' | 12' | 6'-4"

BOARD WIDTH: 4"

PANEL LENGTH: 8' | 4' | 4' | 8'

PANEL WIDTH: 4' | 4' | 4' | 4' | 4' | 2' | 4' | 2' | 8' | 4' | 4' | 2'

top: Exterior cladding details
bottom: Cladding systems layout: horizontal cedar siding pattern above;
vertical cement-board siding pattern below

**top:** Living room view
**right:** Entry view from living room
**opposite:** Kitchen view

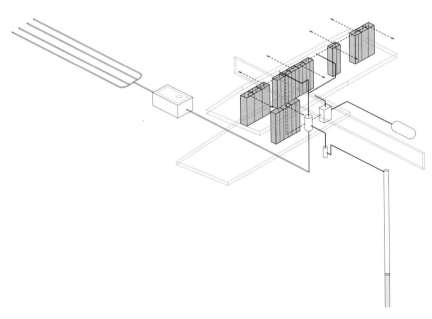

**left:** Second-floor hall view
**top right:** Bedroom view
**middle right:** Bathroom
**bottom:** Infrastructure isometric: plumbing, heating, and cooling runs
**opposite:** Upper-deck view

# VVE House

LOCATION: HURLEY, NEW YORK / PROGRAM: RESIDENTIAL
ORGANIZATION: STATISTICAL / LOCAL CODE: SETTLEMENT PATTERNS
AREA: 2,400 SF / PROPOSAL DATE: 2007

This project is a renovation of a combined garage and cottage building into a weekend residence in upstate New York. The site, a fifty-acre farm consisting of five buildings and various fields, occupies a small portion of a dramatic edge between a steep mountain range and a flat agricultural valley. Along this edge runs a road, several miles long, that strings out a loose grouping of houses and farm structures. These buildings and parcels drift at varying distances from the road, depending on the landscape, farming activity, and building type, describing a rural inventory of farmhouses, garages, barns, silos, and sheds. Like the settlements along the road, the buildings within the fifty-acre parcel have a relationship to one another and to the road based on landscape, proximity, and use. From these drifting settlement patterns along the road and the inventory of residential- and farm-building types, we created a similar pattern of residential program components (kitchen, bathrooms, storage, mechanical, etc). In this regard, a settlement pattern can apply to an urban or a rural context, a plot, or the organization of a building.

Since the budget constraints of the project ruled out building a completely new house or reconfiguring the form of the existing building, we retained as much of the garage/cottage as possible. We determined that the foundation, wood-frame structure, infrastructure, and white-painted wood-slat interior cladding—irregular and out of square as they all were—would remain and that any new element would act as an insertion, independent of the existing building. These elements, as discrete programmatic boxes, drift within and outside the existing structure, defining the living spaces while creating a tension between old and new within the building.

The inventory of these boxes breaks down by function: kitchen cabinetry, containing all appliances and plumbing; two separate bathrooms; mechanical closet; clothes closets; a fireplace and media cabinet; an outdoor barbecue counter; and exterior benches and planter boxes. Each of these boxes falls within the overall drift pattern of the site.

Color and the material-surface palette are important in this scheme as the means of identifying the new elements against the existing renovated structure. Since the existing interior cladding is made of white-painted rough wood slats, running horizontally throughout the interior shell, this backdrop for the new elements is already established in the original building. The new program boxes—clad in a linear, black-stained wood veneer, with vertically oriented grain—stand out against the irregular white boards, while the color of the inside of each volume is a mustard yellow. The materials of these yellow interiors depend on the usage of the box: closet interiors are laminate, the kitchen backsplash is glass, and the bathrooms are tiled. This consistent use of black wood on the exterior and one color on the interior reinforces the identity of the boxes as an inventory of new insertions. Moreover, the black wood of the exterior, along with the existing white-painted wood on the walls, provides a neutral palette that emphasizes the colors of the landscape visible through the windows.

Because the building is a vacation home for time away from the city, views onto the landscape and other farm buildings are prioritized. Using two types of pastoral view—long, sweeping landscape views and close-framed views of rural architecture—we established a set of rules that determine the position of the windows and boxes in relation to the outward views. Interior spaces were organized in response to box and window placement. By maximizing views from specific locations inside the house, windows and boxes are frequently "out of alignment" with one another. Consequently, the shift of boxes and interior spaces can be read from the outside of the building through the pattern of windows. Two dimensions of windows are utilized in the house. Large, eight-foot-by-four-foot door and window openings are placed in relation to the mountain and agricultural views and public spaces of the house (the living, dining, and kitchen areas). Smaller, four-foot-four-by-four-foot-four windows and skylights (doubled and folded in half) are placed in relation to the property, building, and sky views and private spaces of the house (bedroom, study, and bathroom areas). Like the minimal and consistent use of material and color, the use of only two door types and window sizes further emphasizes the reading of an inventory of new insertions (of standard dimension) against an existing (out-of-square) farm building.

Consistency as an approach to revealing difference is continued in the new exterior cladding of the building. Metal siding wraps the entire building and, like the interior wood boxes, covers roof and walls in vertical standing-seam strips that run from foundation to eve to ridge and back down to foundation without a break. This mute wrapping reinforces the idea of the building as a container of inventoried boxes of program and windows with views.

top: Southeast view
bottom left: Drifting settlement patterns along a topographic line
bottom right: Geologic edge between Catskill Mountains and Esopus Creek valley

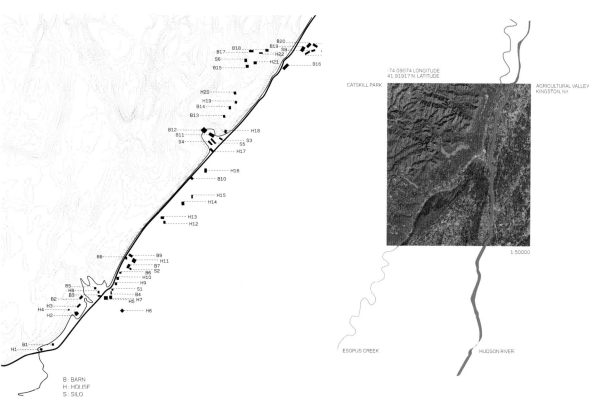

-74.09074 LONGITUDE
41.91917 N. LATITUDE

CATSKILL PARK

AGRICULTURAL VALLEY
KINGSTON, NY

1:50000

ESOPUS CREEK

HUDSON RIVER

B20
B19
B18    H22
B17    S8
S6     H21
B15    H20
       H19
B14    B16
B13

B12
B11    H18
S4     S3
       S5
       H17
       H16
       B10
       H15
       H14
       H13
       H12

B8     B9
       H11
       B7     S2
       B6
       H10
       H9
B5     S1
B8
B2     B4
B3
H3     H5  H7
H4
H2     H6

B1
H1

B : BARN
H : HOUSE
S : SILO

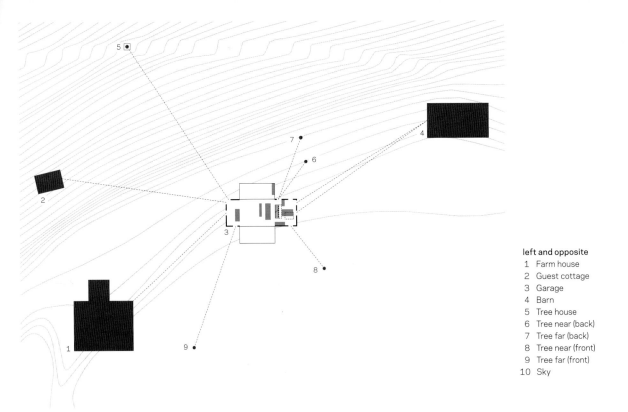

left and opposite
1   Farm house
2   Guest cottage
3   Garage
4   Barn
5   Tree house
6   Tree near (back)
7   Tree far (back)
8   Tree near (front)
9   Tree far (front)
10  Sky

**top:** Site-plan diagram
**bottom:** South view

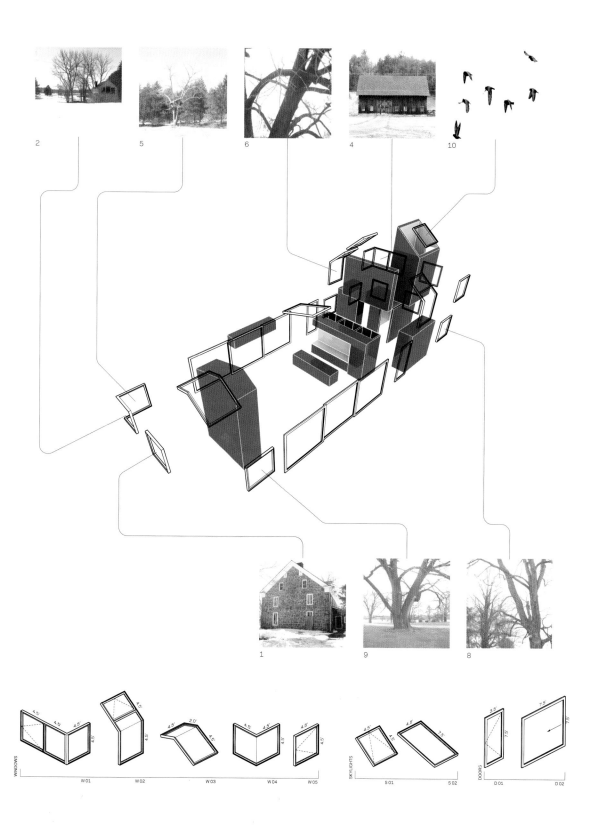

Catalog of views, windows, boxes

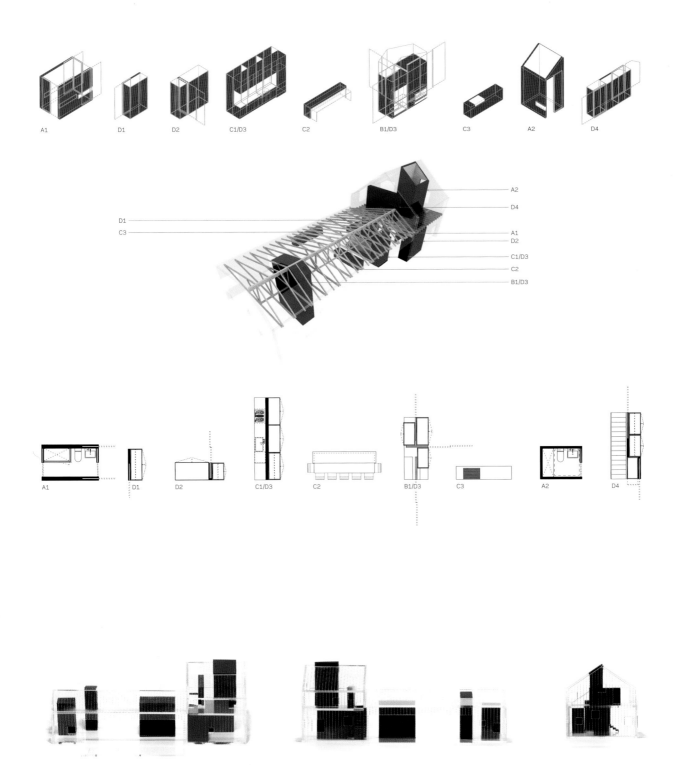

**top:** Study for programmatic boxes within building enclosure
**bottom:** Study model of boxes in building shell

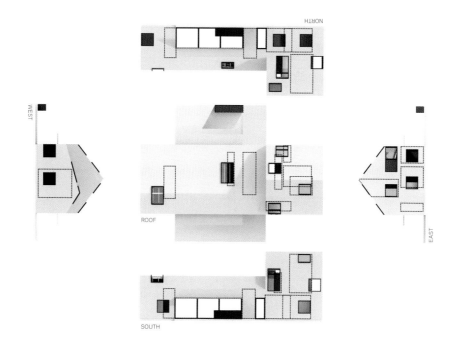

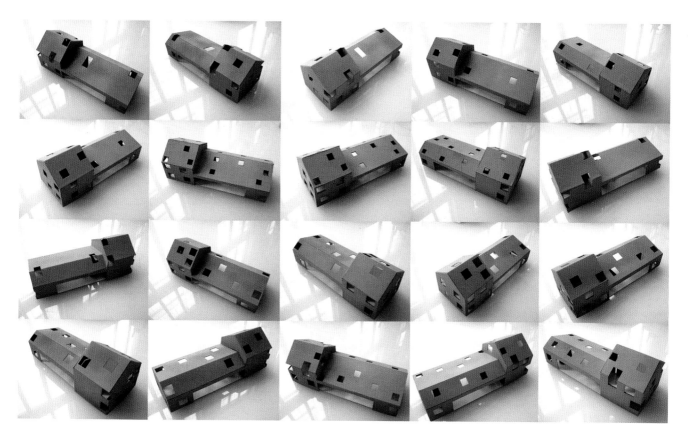

**top:** Unfolded elevation studies
**bottom:** Model studies for apertures

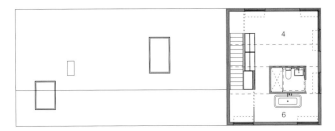

Second-floor plan

1 Entry
2 Kitchen
3 Living
4 Bedroom
5 Study
6 Bathroom
7 Closet / storage
8 Terrace

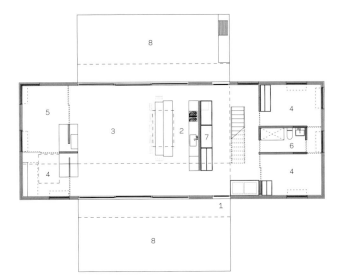

First-floor plan ⌐————————⌐ 15'  ⏱

Programmatic box diagram

top: Second-floor interior view
bottom: Northeast view

# Chelsea Penthouse

LOCATION: NEW YORK, NEW YORK / PROGRAM: RESIDENTIAL
ORGANIZATION: SYNTACTIC / LOCAL CODE: SKYLINE VIEWS
AREA: 1,200 SF / COMPLETION DATE: 2001

This project is the renovation of a twentieth-floor penthouse apartment that faces north and west with views of the Empire State Building. The concept of the project is based on an expanded idea of site. Since the view of this iconic building fills the windows, we wanted to incorporate it into the "site" of the apartment. The simple device of a reflecting glass wall scales, distorts, and doubles the image of the building, making it part of the domestic space of the apartment.

Taking cues from Jacques Tati's movie *Playtime*, in which modern architecture's use of glass as an ephemeral material is validated in the material's reflection of Paris landmarks such as the Eiffel Tower, we use glass to achieve distortion and multiplication in celebration of the "image" of the landmark building. A bent frosted-glass plane slices through the entire width of the apartment; and as anyone who has ever played with two mirrors joined at one end and angled off one another knows, a simple bend with glass can have a powerful effect. The two floor-to-ceiling glass panels bend at a six-degree angle, creating multiple reflections of the images of the Empire State Building. These reflected views are seen best when one is sitting at the dining table with his or her back to the actual view. In this way, everyone sitting at the table can enjoy an actual or reflected view of the Empire State Building.

While acting as a rescaling and doubling device, this glass plane also divides the spaces of the kitchen and the study from the living and dining areas. The frosted-glass wall allows light to pass through to the spaces on either side of it, while it also allows for privacy and separation.

Two floor-to-ceiling storage volumes, positioned perpendicular to each other at opposite ends of the apartment, divide the kitchen from the study and the bedroom from the living area. Both boxes are wrapped in quartersawn ash veneer. As room dividers, in lieu of walls, these storage volumes are accessible from both sides, depending on function and storage requirements. The kitchen-study box, for example, has a refrigerator and a pantry on the kitchen side and a TV, stereo, and bookshelves on the study side. The two densely packed, double-sided storage boxes contain the storage for the apartment, allowing the rest of the space to be open and clutter-free.

Score joints in the concrete floor, a curtain track at the ceiling, and the lighting pattern delineate areas in the open space of the living and dining volumes. When open, the white parachute-fabric curtain rests on its track against the wall between the living and dining rooms; when closed, the curtain creates an informal guest room out of the living area.

The materials throughout the apartment include the frosted-glass wall, ash-wood storage boxes, stainless-steel and aluminum structure, and concrete floors and counters. The kitchen is mostly blue, with auto-body painted cabinet doors above and below. A blue glass backsplash wraps around the entire kitchen, terminating at the breakfast counter, where it runs in front of the glass wall. There, where glass wall meets kitchen counter and backsplash, a casual assembly of materials is used, revealing the layering of program, privacy, and translucency.

  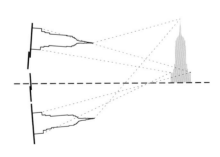

left: *Playtime*, directed by Jacques Tati, 1967
middle: Plan and the city skyline
right: Empire State Building multiple reflection study for bent glass wall
opposite: Reflection of landmark building in glass wall

**top left:** Living room view with parachute curtain open
**top right:** Living room view with parachute curtain closed
**bottom:** Dining room view with glass wall, kitchen, and study beyond

**top and bottom:** Kitchen components: translucent glass wall; blue glass backsplash; cabinets painted with high-gloss blue auto body paint; stainless steel counter support and polished concrete counter

# Cedarhurst Spiral Housing

LOCATION: CEDARHURST, NEW YORK / PROGRAM: RESIDENTIAL
ORGANIZATION: NEURAL / LOCAL CODE: SPIRAL CONFIGURATIONS
AREA: 100,000 SF / PROPOSAL DATE: 2007

This forty-four-unit housing project was designed for a corner site comprising two lots in Cedarhurst, Long Island. The community consists predominantly of Orthodox Jewish and middle-income families, but the site was designated for middle- to lower-income housing where the town's main commercial strip disperses into single- and multifamily housing. On the corner at the end of the secondary street is a large golf course, a primary recreational vector acting on the site. Another important element is the presence of fruit trees at the interior edge of the corner lot, a significant factor for this demographic, since Jewish law forbids the destruction of fruit trees. With the addition of a second lot to the main parcel, the existing trees sit at the center of the newly configured site. Our proposal maintains the location of these trees by creating a central courtyard and spiraling the units of the building around this open space. Though it would not be possible, without moving the trees, to build the project with a garage below, it was agreed that the trees could be temporarily displaced during construction and then replanted in their original location. Interestingly, and further related to the population of the building, the Talmud, which comprises rabbinic interpretations of Jewish law, centers the original text on the page, spiraling around it the discussions of this text throughout time. We found the combination of recreational space, fruit trees, and Jewish law to be worthy of analysis and consideration in this project.

Following these various pattern precedents, the building's organizational scheme describes an ascending spiral that begins below grade in the parking garage and travels up through the building and around the fruit-tree courtyard, disposing duplex units and culminating in the building's common pool. This configuration organizes the building's structure, infrastructure, unit layouts, and green/open space.

Structurally, the building employs a simple concrete column-and-slab system that revolves around the courtyard. Because we employ a stacked-and-shifted skip-stop unit-and-hall scheme (explained below), the columns travel straight up from the ground, and the slabs sit at the floor heights. This stacking also facilitates a very efficient infrastructural layout, whereby utilities are run through the section of the building in a series of walls and risers. Cost efficiency was a continual concern—stressed externally by the client but also internally, within our office, because we wanted to save precious funds for other areas of the building, such as the common pool at the top of the building, which is the culmination of the spiral.

Interior courtyard view with fruit trees

This pool—a cost-intensive area of the building—is also structurally intensive. The columns are set in the center of the portion of the building at the end of the spiral and drop down to split the underground-garage access ramps. The deep concrete beams required to support the pool and cantilever occupy the thickness below the pool, which is afforded by the low head height, in turn made possible by the access ramps.

The apartment units are laid out to stack and spiral like the structural scheme, but the skip-stop section increases the efficiency of the building's construction and usage. A conventional skip-stop scheme eliminates the necessity of a hallway on every floor by using duplex units. In our spiral housing, the building organization is shifted in section to avoid a relentless hallway-and-unit-entry situation. As a result, each floor contains half as many entries, thereby maximizing privacy and intimacy in the building.

The units themselves are simple in their layout of circulation, infrastructure (plumbing and mechanicals), and storage. There are eight different unit types, ranging from single-story studio apartments to two- and three-bedroom duplexes. Finally, the unit aggregate is planned in such a way that combining any two adjacent apartments above, below, or side to side is facilitated by adjacent breaks in structural walls and mechanical chases.

An undefined open space was required by the town code. For us, this was an opportunity for trees and grass, as opposed to paved surfaces, especially in a housing proposal. Three types of green space exist in the project: the individual unit with its private terrace or balcony, the courtyard with its fruit-tree garden, and the street with its public park of trees and planters. Each unit receives green in the form of a private or shared balcony. This is achieved by using the floor-through duplex apartment as a methodology, which provides balconies on the courtyard side for the units that face the interior and balconies toward the street for the units that occupy the corners. This organization of "everyone has access to outdoor space" drives the configuration of the building's surfaces, as well as the courtyard.

The overall form of the building—open at the base for professional offices and more solid above for residential units—creates an inviting street presence, made even more so by the ring of trees and benches along the sidewalk and continuing inward toward the fruit-tree courtyard. The facades of the street-level offices are configured in a repetitive arrangement of aluminum-framed glass storefront modules, while the upper private floors are clad in light-gray fiber-cement panels, whose breaks and pattern follow the window arrangement. The windows of the residential units require more privacy than those on the commercial ground floor; therefore, they have smaller apertures while still providing plenty of light. In this regard, the windows shift and vary, ganged into banks of units to allow as much light as possible to filter into the interior. The windows' irregular rhythm, driven by the interior-unit layouts, creates facades that are varied on all sides. The large recesses of the shared terraces and balconies at the corners of the building facades are clad in charcoal-gray cement panels (as opposed to the light-gray panels on the outside of the building), distinguishing the places in the building where there is a shared outdoor space.

This project configures the typical multifamily apartment-building scheme by using the non-automotive courtyard and the duplex unit as the primary drivers of the building's configuration and morphology. In addition, it posits that a form—the spiral, in this case—can be engaged at various diagrammatic levels to produce an efficient building scheme with a diversity of spaces, units, and effects.

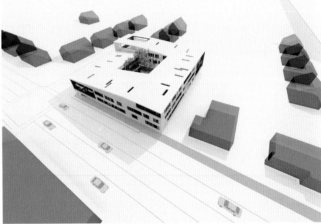

**left:** Site plan
**right:** Aerial view from northwest

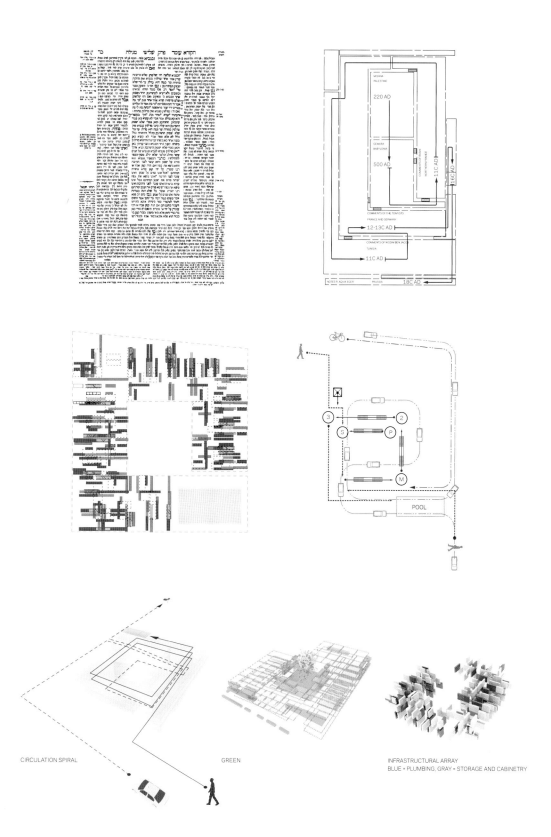

top: Spiral pattern of interpretive texts in the Talmud
middle and bottom: Diagram of spiral circulation and layered infrastructural systems

CIRCULATION SPIRAL

GREEN

INFRASTRUCTURAL ARRAY
BLUE = PLUMBING, GRAY = STORAGE AND CABINETRY

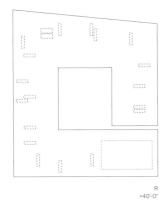

R
+40'-0"

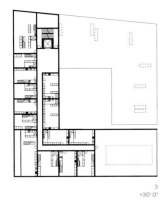

3
+30'-0"

2
+20'-0"

M
+10'-0"

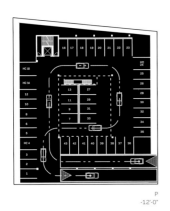

P
-12'-0"

SUB 1
-2'-0"

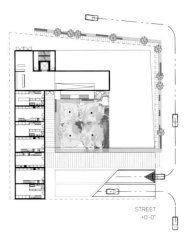

STREET
+0'-0"

Plans

**top:** Northeast view
**bottom left:** Northwest view
**bottom right:** East view

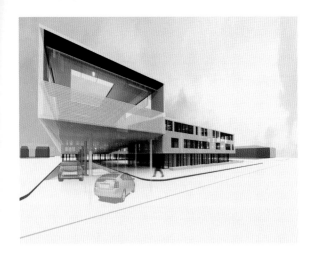

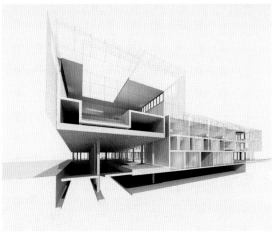

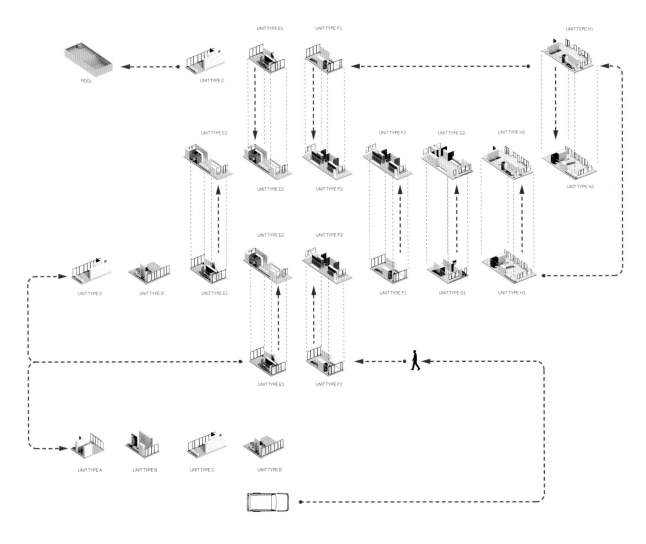

**top left:** Southeast view at auto entry under common pool
**top right:** Section through pool and units
**bottom:** Unit catalog showing methods of access to the individual units

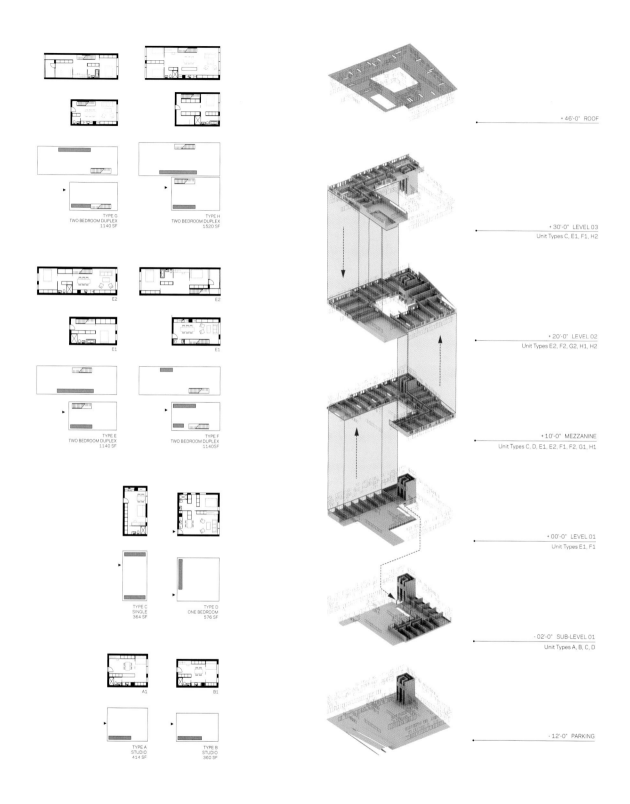

TYPE G
TWO BEDROOM DUPLEX
1140 SF

TYPE H
TWO BEDROOM DUPLEX
1520 SF

E2

E2

E1

E1

TYPE E
TWO BEDROOM DUPLEX
1140 SF

TYPE F
TWO BEDROOM DUPLEX
1140SF

TYPE C
SINGLE
364 SF

TYPE D
ONE BEDROOM
576 SF

A1

B1

TYPE A
STUDIO
414 SF

TYPE B
STUDIO
360 SF

+ 46'-0"  ROOF

+ 30'-0"  LEVEL 03
Unit Types C, E1, F1, H2

+ 20'-0"  LEVEL 02
Unit Types E2, F2, G2, H1, H2

+ 10'-0"  MEZZANINE
Unit Types C, D, E1, E2, F1, F2, G1, H1

+ 00'-0"  LEVEL 01
Unit Types E1, F1

- 02'-0"  SUB-LEVEL 01
Unit Types A, B, C, D

- 12'-0"  PARKING

left: Unit types
right: Floor-plate diagram showing the interlocking of paths of travel to duplex units

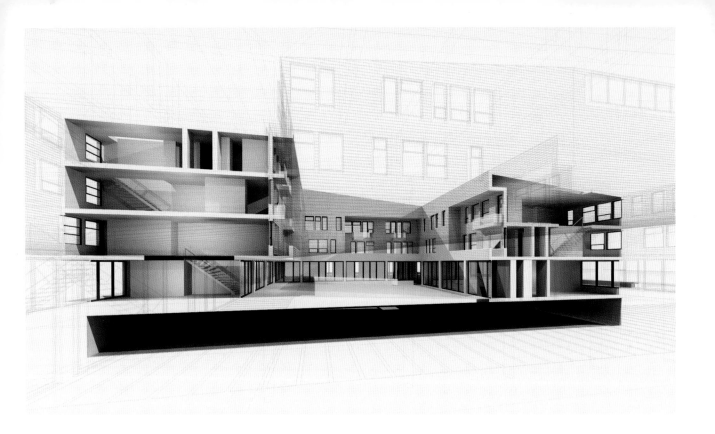

Section through units

**top:** South view
**bottom:** North view from street

# Nassau Street Lobby

LOCATION: NEW YORK, NEW YORK / PROGRAM: RESIDENTIAL
ORGANIZATION: NEURAL / LOCAL CODE: MOVEMENT
AREA: 1,000 SF / COMPLETION DATE: 2002

This project, a lobby for a residential apartment building, is located in downtown Manhattan on a pedestrian street consisting of primarily commercial storefronts. The introduction of a residential program into a busy shopping area prompted a series of responses: to set the lobby facade apart from the commercial facades on the street; to invert the open, transparent street front with a more private entry; to maintain some light and views to and from the street; and to register the bustling pedestrian activity of the street.

At the interface between the street and the interior of the lobby, which is a ten-foot-wide-by-thirteen-foot-high primarily glass facade, the above intentions are achieved by etching and clear-masking the glass panels. Acid-etching most of the glass provides a soft glow of natural light in the space throughout the day while maintaining an intimacy that the neighboring commercial storefronts deny. In order to expose only select views, clear zones are masked out of the etched panels. These two distinct glass treatments blur and frame the frenetic back-and-forth movement of people on the street. The interior of the lobby extends this tactic of capturing movement in the architecture. We see the design of a space as a tracking device for measuring the pace and activity of the individual from the street into the lobby. The methods of tracking these activities are visible in a series of framed and reflected views and in the material joints and horizontal planes of various programs.

The frequent joints in the materials are located to track rhythms and patterns of activity. The score-joint arrangement in the terrazzo floor is a pattern based on the speed of an occupant and the activity being performed within the lobby (entry from street, checking of mail, stopping at the security desk, sitting on the bench, waiting for the elevator). Score joints that have small distances between them represent slower movements, and score joints that have larger distances between them represent faster movements. These lines in the floor continue up the adjacent walls—as breaks in the glass panels in the north wall and as breaks in the cement-board panels in the south wall. This "time code" of lines marks the pace of an individual as he or she moves "in" or "out" of time with the calibrated registration on the walls and floor.

Inside the lobby, the architectural elements track movement and cut images of people passing through the space. The primary element is a glass-paneled wall with horizontally sliced cutouts, which is in front of a mirror that runs the full length of the lobby. The effect is twofold: where the etched glass is in front of the mirror, a subtle reflection of movement is perceived; but at the cutouts, where the mirror is exposed, there is a clear, cropped image of the activity in the lobby. These cutouts align with the clear zones in the street-front glass, shooting framed views out to the street—and are positioned at locations where various activities occur in the lobby. Moreover, the reflection of this glass wall heightens the luminosity in the lobby and gives the small dimension of the space a feeling of greater width.

The detail at the glass-wall cutouts is composed of frosted, low-iron glass panels, which rest on stainless-steel clips that are mounted to the mirrored wall. Thumb-turn fasteners located in front and behind the glass are covered in surgical tubing and act as stops to hold the panels in place.

Complementary to the slicing and marking conditions of the walls and floors in the space are three horizontal volumes: the canopy, which runs from the outside—as an illuminated weather covering—through the mailbox zone and into the reception-desk zone; the reception desk itself; and the waiting bench. Each one of these elements is set at a different height according to its function; and together, like the cuts in the glass wall, they create a condition of fluid back-and-forth movement throughout the space.

**above:** Nassau Street sliced views
**opposite:** Facade entry view

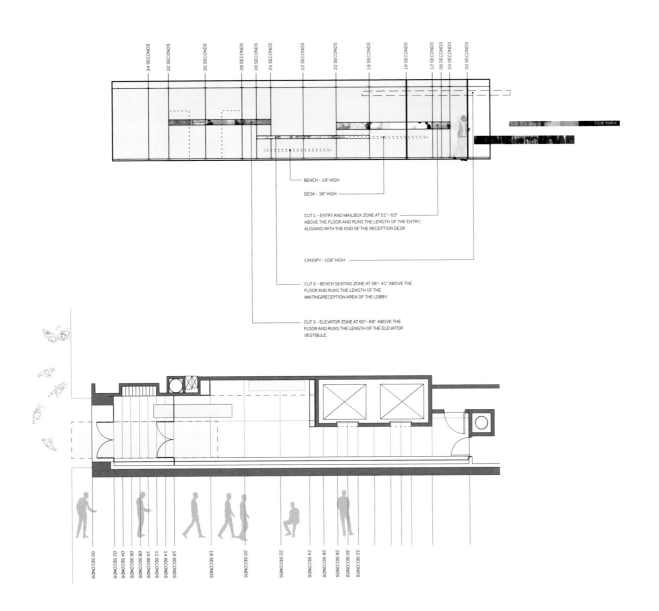

**top:** Glass wall elevation with mirror slots, related programs, and glass joints
**bottom:** Plan with time code

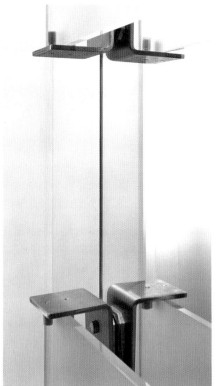

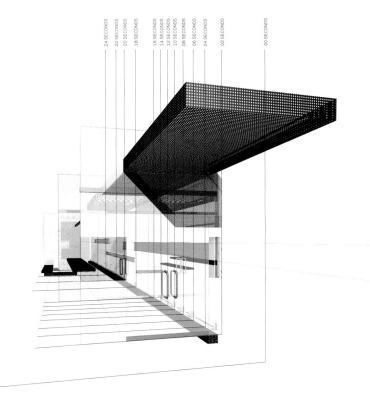

top left: Reception desk passing through glass wall
top right: Canopy, desk, and light fixture passing through glass wall
bottom left: Glass wall made of frosted panels, held in place with stainless steel angles and thumb-turn screw stops, and mirror behind
bottom right: Facade view with time code

**WORK**

# Mixed Greens Gallery

LOCATION: NEW YORK, NEW YORK / PROGRAM: COMMERCIAL
ORGANIZATION: SYNTACTIC / LOCAL CODE: BEAM AND COLUMN
AREA: 3,500 SF / COMPLETION DATE: 2005
IN COLLABORATION WITH GHISLAINE VINAS INTERIOR DESIGN

This project for a gallery in the Chelsea art district of
Manhattan includes two separate exhibition spaces, gallery
offices, and storage, as well as a lounge space for browsing
the gallery's online collection and hanging out during opening
receptions. The space the client secured for the gallery had an
irregular structural condition: a series of large wood columns
and beams, running variably down the middle of the space.
Initially seen as an impediment to the organization, exhibition
layout, and clean mechanical runs, this wiggly line of structure
became the generator of all patterns and configurations in the
design of the gallery. A luminous ceiling, the office and storage-
room walls, and integrated furniture pieces all exist within a
pattern system developed from this beam-and-column
configuration.

Programmatically, the functions of office, storage, and
packing spaces are situated in the middle of the gallery, on
either side of the pre-existing structural geometry of the wood
beams and columns. The central position of these spaces
diverges from the typical gallery organization, whereby storage
space and the main office are concealed. This layout creates
two separate gallery areas, as well as a corridor between these
two galleries. This pinched zone—where the lines of the ceiling
squeeze tightly and then open out into the two galleries—also
functions as the reception area and the connection between
the office and the storage zones.

As one of the few available surfaces for design in an art
gallery that requires white walls, the ceiling condenses all
aspects of the site and program strategies for the gallery in its
lighting, organization, and technology. The form of this luminous ceiling volume—constructed of aluminum flat bar, translucent acrylic, and internal and external lighting—proliferates
the configuration of the existing structure as it moves through
the space in a pattern across the width of the gallery. In addition, the mechanical and sprinkler systems required for the
occupation of the space inhabit this luminous ceiling volume
and penetrate the surface as needed. Occupying the plenum
space created by the dropped ceiling, HVAC ducts run across
the gallery, with linear slot diffusers following the aluminum
lines, supplying warm or cool air to the galleries, office, storage
space, and connecting hall. Finally, sprinkler heads that penetrate the ceiling float as a constellation of points within the
translucent panels. In this way, the ceiling design integrates
all the infrastructural requirements wrapping it all in a light-
filled volume.

Front gallery view

The gallery contains four types of light: ambient light for work spaces; flexible, focused lighting for the display of art; task lighting for particular meeting spaces; and glowing light at the street-front window, as a sign for the gallery. Each lighting type is addressed in distinct ways, and all but the street-front window are integrated into the luminous hung ceiling. The overall ambient light of the main volume comprises fluorescent-light tubes inside an acrylic-and-aluminum volume. These lights are installed above the translucent panels and follow the lines generated from the big wood beam. To achieve the desired even, shadowless glow of the ceiling, the fixtures are positioned far enough away from the panels to avoid hot spots and to separate utility runs from the light as much as possible. The flexible, focused lighting is achieved throughout the gallery by attaching the lighting tracks to the sides of the aluminum bars that hold the acrylic in place. Thus integrated into the glowing ceiling, the track lighting also follows the wiggle of the ceiling pattern. The lines of the track lighting continue from the glowing ceiling and are grooved into the flat ceiling beyond the central volume to provide display lighting to the two main gallery spaces. The task-light fixtures, called tailLights, also extend out from the ceiling volume. These fixtures drop below or stretch beyond the plane of the ceiling to illuminate and highlight the entry, reception desk, office conference area, pivoting media table, bathroom, and bar/lounge area. Considered an extension of the lines in the ceiling pattern, the tailLights are fabricated according to the same aluminum flat bar. Finally, there is the green glow behind the street-facade window, which is the one lighting type not associated with the ceiling; its color signals the name and presence of the gallery in the neighborhood.

Three large integrated furniture pieces—the reception desk, pivoting media table, and bar—follow the formal language of the ceiling and extend through the space in long cantilevers and articulating pivots. Each piece is the central focus of the space it inhabits, addressing distinct programmatic desires in the gallery. And as a result of their necessities, each piece performs in a particular way. The reception desk juts out from the office wall and opens to the entry. The media table contains laptops for browsing the gallery's collection on the website and pivots as needed, depending on the event, the installation, or the time of day. In this regard, the visitor interacts with the gallery at this table, both physically and digitally. Last, the long bar cantilevers into the lounge area as a centerpiece for openings and parties. Structurally, all three pieces are supported at a fixed, or pivoting, end and shoot out along the lines of the light fixtures above. Steel frames clad in painted aluminum panels form the basic support, while each piece contains a specific apparatus for its operation. The most structurally and technically intensive of the three pieces, the pivoting table, utilizes two crane pivots with integral bearings for its movement side to side. This piece additionally incorporates electricity and data ports into its top surface for the use of laptop computers. The laptops can be concealed beneath lids that are hinged at the desk surface like airplane-wing flaps. The seventeen-foot-long bar supports the longest cantilever, extending eleven feet out into the space. It also integrates plumbing and electricity, for the running of the dishwasher and bar sink.

Color is used sparingly but intentionally in this project. The idea of the "white box" gallery space is taken to extremes as white exists in several degrees of gloss and glow. It is also a backdrop to green. The gallery's name, "Mixed Greens," directed the color concept, according to which several shades of green are used in specific locations. Color in this project distinguishes art wall and non-art wall, public and private, and outside and inside space: white corresponds to art walls in galleries, public spaces, and outside surfaces; while green corresponds to non-art walls in offices, work spaces, inside cabinetry, and bathrooms. Additionally, green is the glow behind the front windows.

**left:** Facade view with green glow
**right:** Existing beam and columns before renovation

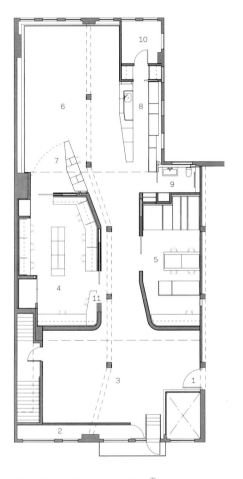

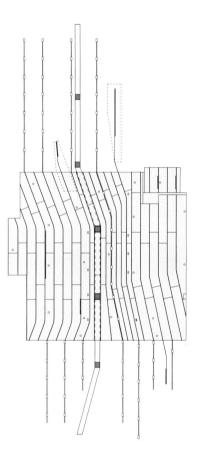

Floor plan ⌐————————⌐ 15'  ⊕        Reflected ceiling plan

1  Entry
2  Display window
3  Front gallery
4  Office
5  Storage/packaging area
6  Rear gallery
7  Pivoting media desk
8  Bar
9  WC
10  Mechanical
11  Reception desk

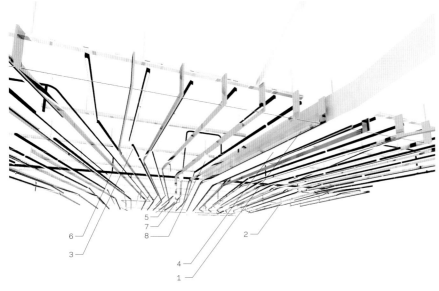

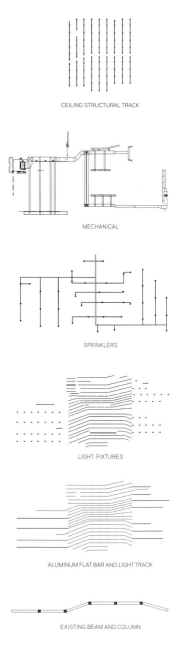

CEILING STRUCTURAL TRACK

MECHANICAL

SPRINKLERS

LIGHT FIXTURES

ALUMINUM FLAT BAR AND LIGHT TRACK

EXISTING BEAM AND COLUMN

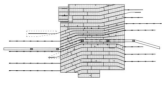

REFLECTED CEILING PLAN COMPOSITE

1 Aluminum flat bar
2 TailLight
3 Acrylic panel
4 Existing beam
5 Fluorescent tube
6 Sprinkler system
7 Hanging rods
8 Light fixture

**top left:** Construction photo of fluorescent lights at ceiling
**middle left:** Ceiling assembly drawing
**right, top to bottom:** Ceiling components
**opposite:** Entry view toward office

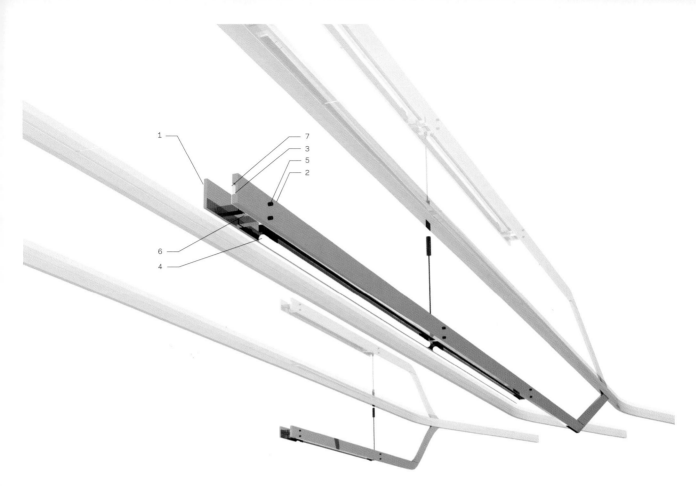

1  1/4" x 2" mill finish aluminum bar
2  1/2" x 2" bar milled for 1/16" plate and grooves for wire
3  Wiring groove
4  "Nippo" t5 fluorescent light fixture, reassemble within custom aluminum bar assembly
5  #10 stainless steel socket-head cap screw
6  1/2" x 1 mill finish aluminum rod frilled and tapped for #10 screws
7  1/16" x 2" mill finish aluminum bar

TailLight details

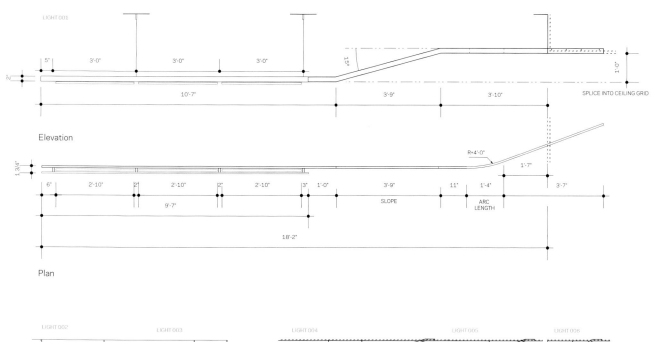

LIGHT 001

Elevation

Plan

LIGHT 002    LIGHT 003    LIGHT 004    LIGHT 005    LIGHT 006

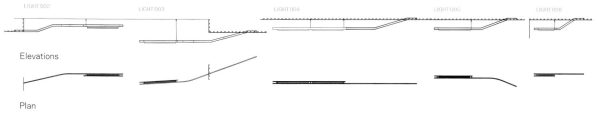

Elevations

Plan

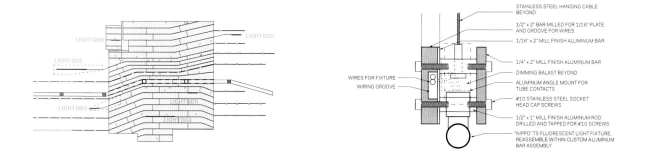

LIGHT 006                    LIGHT 002
LIGHT 001
LIGHT 005
LIGHT 003            LIGHT 004

STAINLESS STEEL HANGING CABLE
BEYOND

1/2" x 2" BAR MILLED FOR 1/16" PLATE
AND GROOVE FOR WIRES

1/16" x 2" MILL FINISH ALUMINUM BAR

1/4" x 2" MILL FINISH ALUMINUM BAR

DIMMING BALAST BEYOND

ALUMINUM ANGLE MOUNT FOR
TUBE CONTACTS

WIRES FOR FIXTURE

WIRING GROOVE

#10 STAINLESS STEEL SOCKET
HEAD CAP SCREWS

1/2" x 1" MILL FINISH ALUMINUM ROD
DRILLED AND TAPPED FOR #10 SCREWS

"NIPPO" T5 FLUORESCENT LIGHT FIXTURE,
REASSEMBLE WITHIN CUSTOM ALUMINUM
BAR ASSEMBLY

**top:** TailLight elevations and plans
**bottom left:** RCP key plan
**bottom right:** Section detail

Translucent acrylic sliding door with aluminum-flat-bar
handle and slot details

Cantilevered bar counter with tailLight above and green
cabinet interior behind

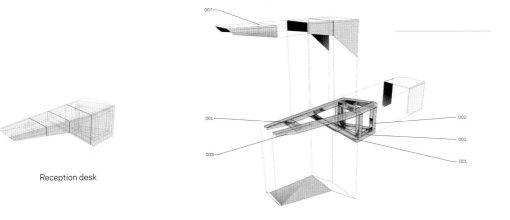

Reception desk

001  6 X 4 STEEL TUBE

002  4 X 4 STEEL POST, TYP.

003  TAPERED 6 X 4 TUBE STEEL

007  PAINTED 1/8" ALUMINUM SHEET PANEL
WITH 3" RADIUSED CORNER, TYP.

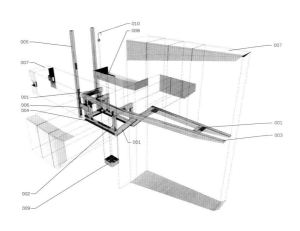

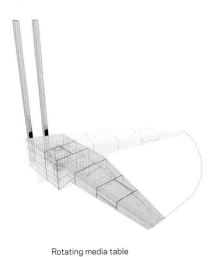

Bar

001  6 X 4 STEEL TUBE

002  4 X 4 STEEL POST, TYP.

003  TAPERED 6 X 4 TUBE STEEL

004  W6 X 12 BEAM

005  4 X 4 X 3/8 STEEL TUBE BOLTED
TO STEEL PLATE TOP  AND BOTTOM

006  STEEL TUBE ATTACHMENT
STRUCTURE, TYP.

007  PAINTED 1/8" ALUMINUM SHEET PANEL
WITH 3" RADIUSED CORNER, TYP.

008  COUNTERTOP SURFACE

009  SINK

010  FAUCET

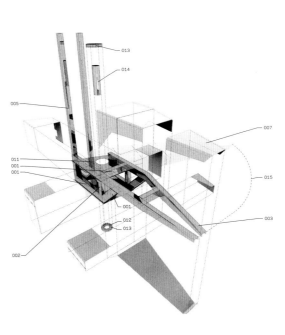

Rotating media table

001  6 X 4 STEEL TUBE

002  4 X 4 STEEL POST, TYP.

003  TAPERED 6 X 4 TUBE STEEL

005  4 X 4 X 3/8 STEEL TUBE BOLTED
TO STEEL PLATE TOP  AND BOTTOM

007  PAINTED 1/8" ALUMINUM SHEET PANEL
WITH 3" RADIUSED CORNER, TYP.

011  1/4" ALUMINUM PLATE BOLTED
TO OUTER TURNTABLE RING
TOP AND BOTTOM

012  INNER TURNTABLE RING
WELDED TO STEEL PLATE
EMBEDDED IN SUBFLOOR

013  OUTER TURNTABLE RING
BOLTED TO 1/4" ALUMINUM
PLATE TOP AND BOTTOM

014  5 5/16" STEEL CYLINDER
WELDED TO INNER
TURNTABLE RING

015  TURNING RADIUS

Fabricated steel and aluminum furniture pieces

  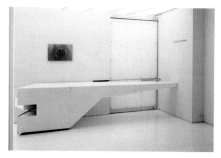

**top:** Rear gallery view
**bottom:** Pivoting media table: powder-coated aluminum and flip-up laptop lids

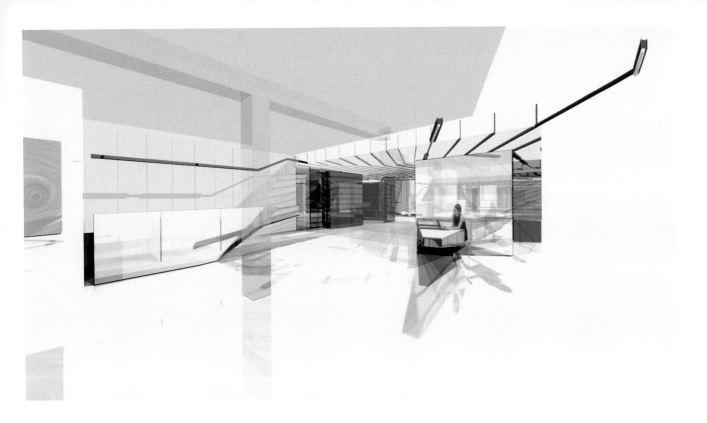

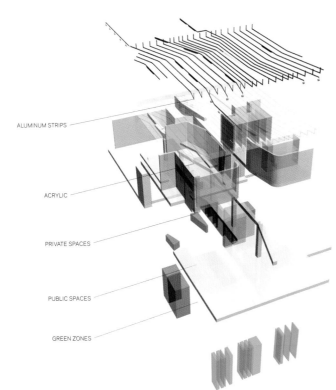

ALUMINUM STRIPS

ACRYLIC

PRIVATE SPACES

PUBLIC SPACES

GREEN ZONES

**top:** Rear gallery perspective view
**bottom:** Pulled-apart isometric showing program, ceiling components, and color

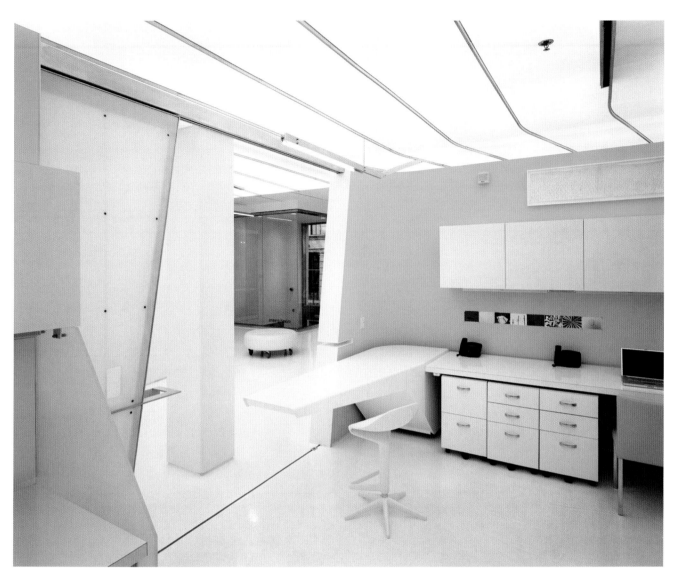

top: Interior office view
bottom: Green bathroom interior

# Stockholm Public Library Addition

LOCATION: STOCKHOLM, SWEDEN / PROGRAM: INSTITUTIONAL
ORGANIZATION: SYNTACTIC / LOCAL CODE: SOLID/VOID
AREA: 250,000 SF / COMPETITION DATE: 2006

This project is an addition to Erik Gunnar Asplund's 1928 Stockholm Public Library. An international competition invited designs for the expansion of the library to hold more volumes and departments, while reconsidering the concept of an urban public library at the beginning of the twenty-first century. When the Stockholm Library was constructed, it gave form to the idea of education and literacy as necessities for Swedish national identity, at once a very local and very national idea. In our design, the library addition is configured around an expanded idea of publicness, where local conditions, the existing library, the park, and the city are reflected in the scheme, but the view is outward in all directions.

The existing Stockholm Library organizes books, reading, offices, and circulation around a cylindrical rotunda illuminated by clerestory windows. This centralized space and its stripped-down classical language formalized the idea of a literate national populace. For our addition to the iconic building, we examined this luminous central space and transformed it into a series of yellow-glass light voids that also carry heating, cooling, and ventilation. In this regard, we transform the classically central-ized void into a new idea of public space based on a sustainable and multicentered organizational system.

A close analysis of the site revealed that the solid-to-void relationship of the urban fabric displays a similar condition to that of the existing library in that the street walls are largely continuous (like the ancillary library spaces) and the courtyards of the blocks are voids (like the rotunda). This analogous pattern condition extends outward to the geological condition of Stockholm and its surrounding islands, as their land (solid) and water (void) distribution form an inversion of the city's pattern.

The section of the immediate site offers several non-traditional possibilities for access into the library. The competi-tion site for the addition is between the park of Observatory Hill above and the city streets and nearby subway station below. This site condition presents the possibility of creating urban landscape and architecture with several points of entry and several paths through the building. Our project takes advantage of this section and allows the landscape and the city to flow up and down, as well as in and through, the building, configuring a porous architecture.

Our design for the addition addresses the site's urban adjacencies by presenting to the city side of the site a transpar-ent street wall with interior glowing yellow volumes and, on the upper hill of the site, paths of circulation connecting back into the park. The nature-to-building connection is reinforced by the extension of the park onto the undulating roof of the library at the south side of the site. Two slots, with stairs that connect to the street below, occur at the roof and cut into the building at this level: The first is located at the upper amphitheater plaza, where the main interior stair of the library connects to the entry plaza below. The second is located at the private garden slot, and it contains an outdoor skinny stair that descends to the partially covered entry courtyard. The park also slips past these two entry connections and travels up onto a series of linear "hills" that are configured by the library departments within the building below. These "hills" are planted and paved for public usage at various scales and concentrations of people. The roof park is always accessible through the building's two twenty-four-hour stairways—one interior and grand (leading up to the amphitheater), the other exterior and linear (a shortcut from city to park).

Since the addition defines the public building as a porous filter for universal access, there are several entries into the library. Two primary public plazas expand these entries. The plaza at the top of the hill foregrounds access to the top floor and onto the roof garden, and the covered, street-level plaza provides entry to the main door and interior public space of the building. Additionally, access from underground and the subway station pops up into this main space. Circulation through the interior of the building can occur between the two plazas (and there can be twenty-four-hour passage through the building), as well as on the exterior stair that runs between the park at the top of the hill and the street-level plaza.

While the design strives to make the building a sectional filter between city and park and to connect the building to the landscape of the park, the building also hovers over the street-level plaza and shoots out of the hill. Just as in the section of the Stockholm Library, the upper two floors of the addition are elevated from the street level. This creates an easy connection between the two buildings. Since the addition dispenses with the solid base, however, a new structural condition is required. The addition employs a series of floor-height Vierendeel trusses that run perpendicular to the hill and rest on columns that step around the subway tunnel and cantilever out toward the street. The result is an infill building with an open base—an urban filter for people and landscape to enter and pass through.

opposite top: Street-level view toward entry
opposite bottom: Elevated view along street

The nine light voids at the core of each of the departments of the addition are designed as yellow double-layered glass volumes. Penetrating the floor plates of the building, they organize all the departments of the library, just as the central rotunda does in the original library. These nine holes also allow for views that shoot through the building, so that from the street or from any department within the library, one can see the sky and often the park. These light voids pull the natural light into the building by stretching out the long way from the southern sun. The severe angle of the winter sun forces light deep into the building. And when lit artificially at night, the light voids glow back toward the city, making the library a public attraction.

Tapping into the district's geothermal heating and cooling, the light voids are an integral infrastructural component of the building's mechanical system. Between the two layers of glass, the light voids take in fresh air and, through the plenum space of the floor plates, supply heating and cooling to the conditioned spaces of the library. In this way, each skylight is a heating and cooling tower within the building.

The glass of the light voids has obviously been selected for its transparency and light-carrying properties, but the yellow color of the glass is part of the "local code" of the city. Many buildings in Stockholm are surfaced in yellow plaster, an attempt to keep the city bright in the middle of the dark winter. In our proposal, the yellow glass internalizes this condition and creates focal points at the many departmental centers against the neutral white-and-gray palette of the rest of the building. At different times of the day and at night, this constellation of yellow voids reflects on the surface of the plaza below, creating pools of yellow light.

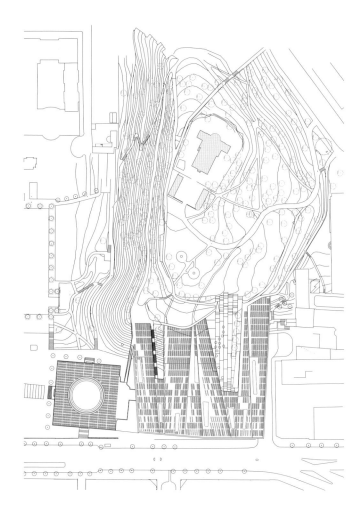

LAND AND WATER IN STOCKHOLM ISLAND CHAIN

CITY BLOCK, SOLID TO VOID

IMMEDIATE NEIGHBORHOOD, SOLID VOID

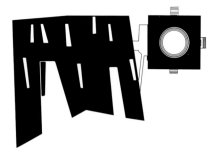

EXISTING LIBRARY AND NEW ADDITION, SKYLIGHT SOLID VOID

top: Site plan
bottom: Solids and voids at various scales

Aerial city view with library and addition proposal

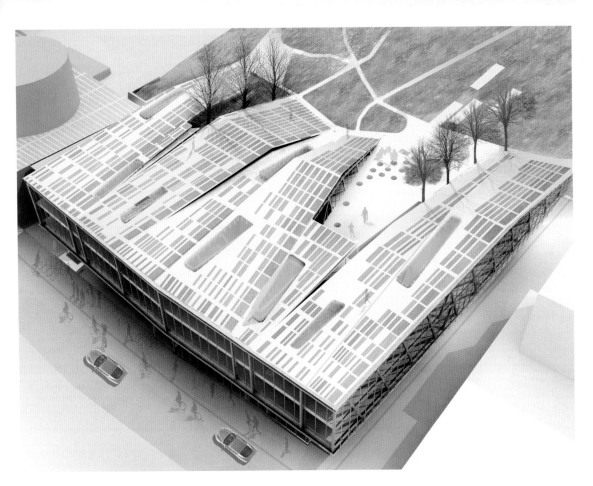

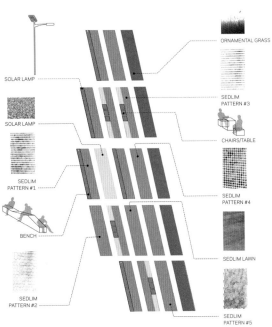

SOLAR LAMP

SOLAR LAMP

SEDLIM
PATTERN #1

BENCH

SEDLIM
PATTERN #2

ORNAMENTAL GRASS

SEDLIM
PATTERN #3

CHAIRS/TABLE

SEDLIM
PATTERN #4

SEDLIM LAWN

SEDLIM
PATTERN #5

**top:** Roof view
**bottom:** Roof park components

**top:** Third-level plan with roof amphitheater and entry from park
**middle:** Second-level plan with connection to Asplund Library
**bottom:** Ground-level plan with entry from street

50'

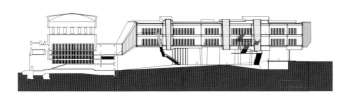

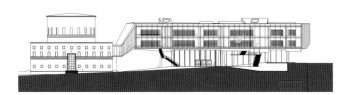
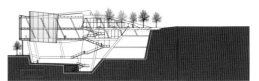

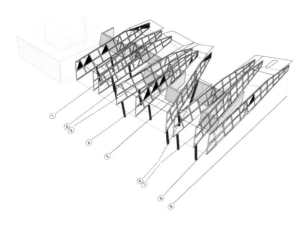

**top:** Model
**middle:** Elevations and sections
**bottom:** Structural diagram: nine Vierendeel trusses perpendicular to hill

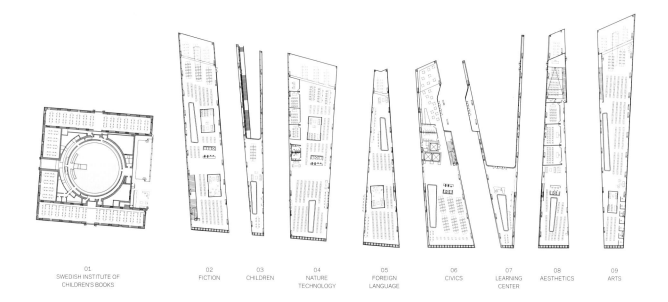

01
SWEDISH INSTITUTE OF
CHILDREN'S BOOKS

02
FICTION

03
CHILDREN

04
NATURE
TECHNOLOGY

05
FOREIGN
LANGUAGE

06
CIVICS

07
LEARNING
CENTER

08
AESTHETICS

09
ARTS

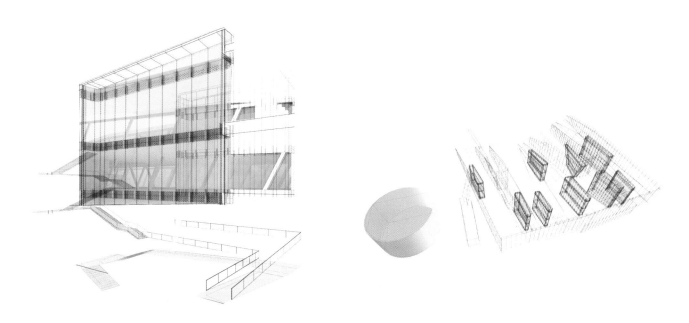

**top:** Pulled-apart library organization diagram: nine departments, nine skylights
**bottom, left and right:** Yellow light void diagrams

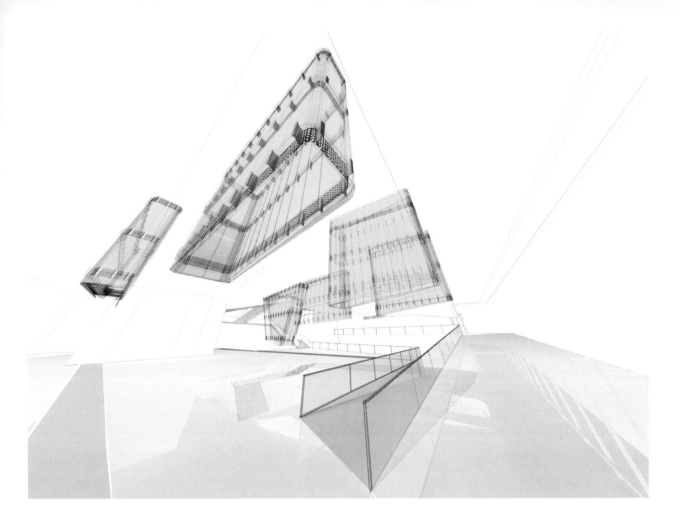

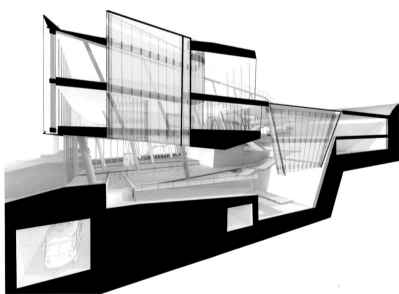

top: View from lower entry with skylights above
bottom: Section perspective drawing, showing cut through subway, access tunnel to subway, ground-floor entry plaza, two skylights, and park-entry amphitheater

**top:** Main-entry view from Asplund Library
**bottom:** Interior view at upper-level entry

# Les Migrateurs Furniture Showroom

**LOCATION: NEW YORK, NEW YORK / PROGRAM: COMMERCIAL**
**ORGANIZATION: STATISTICAL / LOCAL CODE: DISPLAY METHODS**
**AREA: 3,500 SF / COMPLETION DATE: 2002**

This project is located in downtown Manhattan, in the street and basement levels of an old 1850s tea storage building. The client wanted to have the showroom on both floors; but the existing basement had low ceilings and no natural light, so it was dark and uninviting. In order to make a properly illuminated two-story showroom that would invite customers to visit the lower level, it was imperative to open apertures to the basement space.

The most important objective in designing any furniture showroom is the display of objects for sale. How will these pieces be presented, and what do they show? In a typical furniture store, the pieces are placed on the floor for viewing at eye level. But what if the pieces are displayed in such a way that one could view them from above and below as well? How might that affect the shopping experience?

A strategy of cuts in the floor and ceiling offers a way both to bring light to the lower level and to display the furniture in an unconventional manner. Playing on the removal of portions of a floor to enable views from above and below in Gordon Matta-Clark's *Bronx Floors: Floor Above, Ceiling Below*, we made three cutouts, each providing a different method of display.

The three holes are all located within a floor pattern that is inscribed at the street level and sublevel of the store. At the two major termini of the pattern are mirrored panels that reflect back toward the city and the sales desk. This simple floor pattern in the showroom is derived from a compression of the city grid and extends out of the store and onto the sidewalk. The floor pattern serves as a locating apparatus for not only the cutouts, but also the visitor to the store.

Color is used sparingly as a way to foreground the furniture pieces and the visitors. Primarily white, the store is crisscrossed by the beige locating pattern described above. In addition, the use of clear glass and acrylic dematerializes the structure and platforms where the pieces sit, making them appear to float in the space.

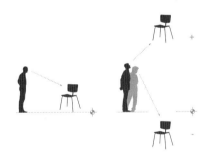

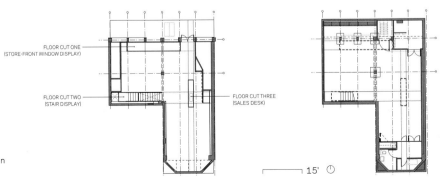

**above, top to bottom:** Layered floor pattern perspective, street facade, viewing methods diagram
**bottom, left to right:** Street-level plan, basement-level plan
**opposite:** View from under storefront display

15'

## Floor Cut One: Storefront Display

This cut, at a dimension of three feet six inches wide and twenty feet long, has a laminated structural glass floor. These transparent floor panels allow furniture pieces to be viewed and inspected from below, as well as from above. Passersby on the street can see down into the lower level, and visitors to the showroom can see up to the street. The cut permits natural light to penetrate from the street level down into the lower level of the showroom and workspace. At night, the lower level of the store glows upward onto the street.

## Floor Cut Two: Stair Display

This cut, at a dimension of three feet wide and sixteen feet eight inches long, has a floating acrylic display platform. The platform allows a select few pieces to be viewed from all perspectives by the visitor who is walking up or down the stairs. At the back wall of the stair opening, there is a full-height two-story mirror, which reflects the backside of the floating platform and allows the visitor to see back to the sales desk as he or she walks down the stair.

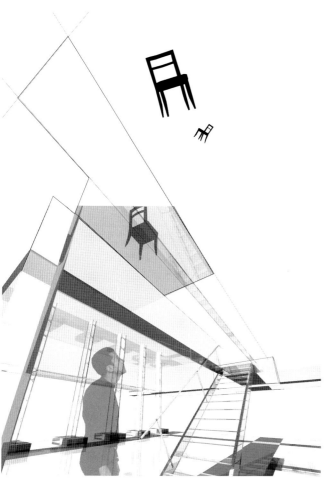

## Floor Cut Three: Sales Desk

This cut, at a dimension of two feet wide and ten feet long, incorporates a transparent and translucent sales desk. Slotted into the cutout in the floor, it is translucent along its long faces and transparent along the top and at its two ends. The desk holds the necessary wiring for all sales equipment, including the computer, the credit-card machine, and the telephone. If one stands below the desk on the lower level, one can observe the sales transactions occurring above.

These three display devices all depend on the cuts in the floor plate for their unorthodox views—of the undersides of furniture and of the people passing through the store, the lower showroom, and back out to the city. In this way, the showroom becomes a highly orchestrated viewing and shopping experience, where the visitor is an active participant in the architecture and the exhibition of merchandise, while the very act of buying and selling is on display.

bottom right: Detail view from below sales desk

# EMR Printing Plant

LOCATION: NEW YORK, NEW YORK / PROGRAM: COMMERCIAL
ORGANIZATION: NEURAL / LOCAL CODE: CIRCUIT/CIRCULATION
AREA: 13,000 SF / COMPLETION DATE: 2000

This project is located in midtown Manhattan on two floors of a commercial building. The client asked us to reorganize the ground floor of its existing plant around a new printing press; to coordinate all new and relocated machinery (including mechanical and electrical requirements); to consolidate several departments into the basement space; and, finally, to create a design that would position the press as an atypical facility in the shrinking world of Manhattan printing.

From the beginning, it was apparent that a significant part of our task would be creating a successful organizational system for the facility. Since the extensive technical requirements for the machinery of the facility overlapped repeatedly with the circulation of materials and people, the design of the space would have to be heavily invested in the network connection of the equipment and people. The fifty to sixty pieces of machinery—all requiring various combinations of electricity, data, water, cooling, ventilation, and humidity control—would have to function simply and efficiently for the project to be successful. In addition, since the printing process from layout to printed matter is essentially an assembly of production, the sequencing and adjacency of departments would be important. In response to these requirements, we created a spatial circuit diagram that organizes the machines, mechanical and electrical equipment, delivery systems, and departments. Because the facility is on two floors, there is a vertical connection—a circulation space, containing a stair and a bridge, devoid of all the bustling activity of machinery, printing, and departments. This zone also serves as the central conduit for all mechanical and electrical access and output in the facility. In other words, everything in the plant either plugs into or moves through this central circuit/circulation space.

This eighty-foot-long-by-five-foot-wide cut in the plate of the ground floor of the building delivers light deep into the various departments through twenty-five foot-high translucent walls. The glow of these walls is created with fluorescent tubes at the exposed ceiling and screened back wall that follow the lines of the stair's supporting beams. This element of light is important, since half the facility is located below ground level. All the plant's departments feed into this glowing space, which begins at the street and extends through both floors to the rear of the building.

Within this illuminated volume, two different conditions of light are used. Inside the circulation space, the light is bright, whereas outside this central zone, the walls glow with a soft, ambient light that diffuses into the workspaces. This central light box, visible from the street, is the identity of the project. It is the primary intervention, the center of the circuit diagram, the motherboard of the neural network.

Prioritizing movement up, down, in, and through the glowing volume, the design of the stair and bridge is crucial as a centerpiece of the space. These two related constructions refine the industrial nature of the plant and the neighborhood through their materials and detailing. The stair structure is made of a painted steel tube that is cut open to make fixing points out of clip details at the floor. The treads and bridge surface are made of aluminum bar grating. The two parts are connected with a tenon joint that slips between the bars of the grating and is fastened with a machine screw through the face of the aluminum. This detail allows the two elements, stringers and treads, to require no intermediate members, which would have made the construction heavier in weight and appearance and more expensive to build. Moreover, since the presence of this zone is established through luminosity, the stair and bridge must be porous, so that light can pass down to the lower level. The figures of the stair and bridge pass through the space and drop out of the bottom of the glowing walls. When underneath the stair or bridge, one can see the shadows of feet as people move through the space.

In a press facility, where print quality and color matching are the stock-in-trade of the business, the color palette of the spaces has to be handled carefully so as not to interfere with the perception of color on the printed material. As a result, the material in the plant is mute in all areas where color checking is to take place. To this end, the palette and materials of the project are primarily white (painted walls and cabinetry), gray (aluminum and concrete), and glow (translucent polycarbonate and acrylic panels). The only areas that receive any color are the lunchroom and the conference area—two spaces that join to make a large company gathering space. Playing off the glowing translucent polycarbonate of the circulation walls, these communal spaces are connected by a blue rubber floor, fir-plywood panels, and translucent green cabinetry for the kitchen and conference area.

opposite: Circulation space

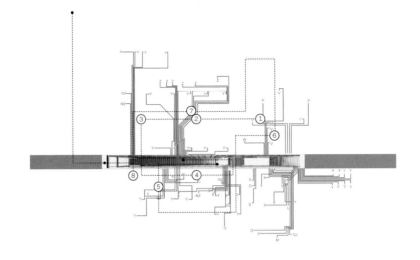

right and opposite:

1  Scanning dept.
2  Desktop publishing dept.
3  Layout stations
4  Production/pre-press
5  Film output dept.
6  Press rooms
7  Bindery dept.
8  Shipping and receiving

A   match-print laminator
B   match-print laminator
C   match-print laminator
D   match-print large frame
E   digital press
F   match-print processor
G   PolaProof
H   PolaProof
I   PolaProof laminator
J   press workstation
K   Delta processor
L   Delta processor
M   Delta PC / Dolev PV
N1  large light table
N2  large light table
O   small frame
P   press
Q   frame processor
R   match-print small frame
S   small light table
T   power pack
U   hell chroma graph
V   hell chroma light station
W   soft-view light table
X   silver recovery unit
Y   workstation
Z   computer processor

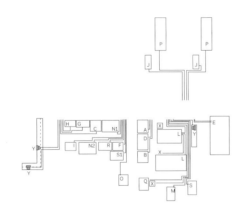

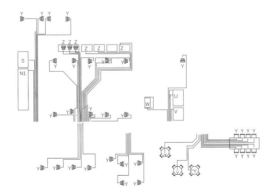

Equipment circuitry diagrams

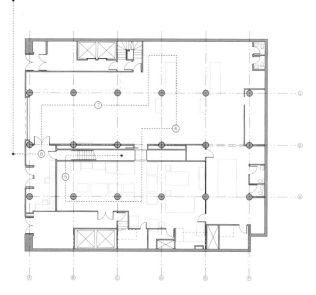

Lower-level plan ⌐———————┐ 15' ⊘                 Street-level plan

top: Plans with department organization
middle left: Film processing department view
bottom left: Lower-level lunchroom and conference room views
right: Desktop publishing

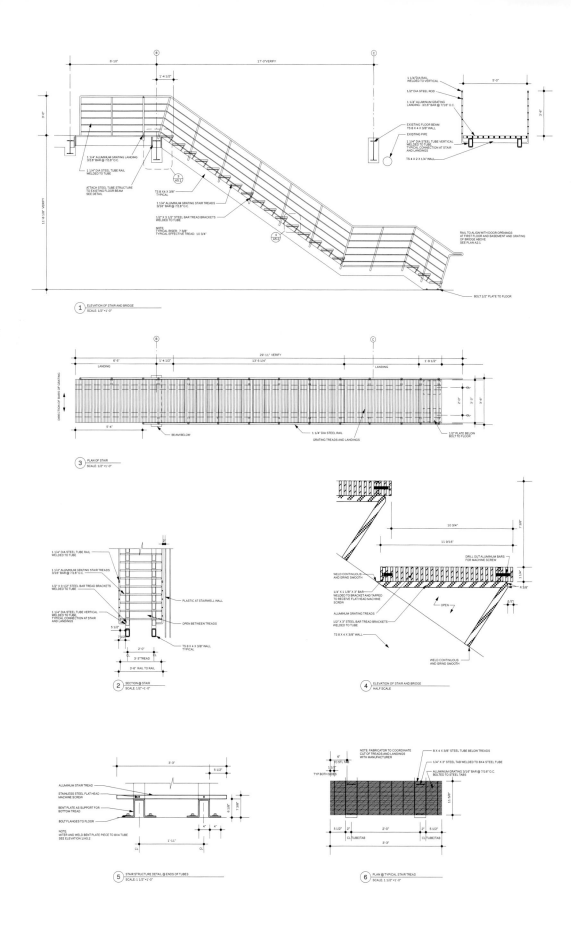

ELEVATION OF STAIR AND BRIDGE
1    SCALE: 1/2" = 1'-0"

3    PLAN OF STAIR
     SCALE: 1/2" = 1'-0"

2    SECTION @ STAIR
     SCALE: 1/2" = 1'-0"

4    ELEVATION OF STAIR AND BRIDGE
     HALF SCALE

5    STAIR STRUCTURE DETAIL @ ENDS OF TUBES
     SCALE: 1 1/2" = 1'-0"

6    PLAN @ TYPICAL STAIR TREAD
     SCALE: 1 1/2" = 1'-0"

opposite: Stair plans, elevations, and details
top left: Lower-level lunchroom
top right and bottom: Stair detailed views

5 ⊙ ---- FILM OUTPUT DEPARTMENT

4 ⊙ ---- PRODUCTION / PRE-PRESS DEPARTMENT

2 ⊙ 1 ⊙ DESKTOP AND SCANNING DEPARTMENTS

**top:** Bridge views from below
**bottom:** Rendered view of stair
**opposite:** Stair from below

**SHOW**

# Site Lines / Line Weights

LOCATION: NEW YORK, NEW YORK, AND AUSTIN, TEXAS / PROGRAM: EXHIBITIONS
ORGANIZATION: STATISTICAL / LOCAL CODE: DIMENSION AND SCALE
AREA: 950 AND 2000 SF / COMPLETION DATE: 2006

In one week in February 2006, two separate solo shows of our work were exhibited at two different schools of architecture: Parsons the New School for Design, in New York City; and the School of Architecture at the University of Texas at Austin. Each show presented eight of our recent projects—the same eight projects for both shows.

Not surprisingly—and true to the respective spatial stereotypes of New York City and Texas—the gallery spaces of the two exhibitions are significantly different. The small gallery space in Manhattan is also an active, uncontained circulation space—essentially a public hallway that feeds an elevator, a stairwell, an administration office, studio spaces, classrooms, and a lecture room. The gallery in Austin is, in contrast, a large room whose sole function is to exhibit work.

Our time and cost constraints were tight for the two shows. One solution might have been to print out boards of the eight projects to be exhibited and simply hang them on the wall. However, we were interested in how these two gallery spaces functioned within the two schools and wanted to create installations that were not only display devices for our work, but also, and more important, spatial responses to the galleries themselves. We were, moreover, interested in the opportunity of having two shows in two different spaces that could together reveal qualities and conditions that a single show might not offer. In this sense, the two shows could be considered as one show in two locations.

Out of this desire to address the two different spatial conditions arose several challenges. First, since the budget and the time for fabrication were limited for both shows, we needed to devise an economical construction procedure. The solution was a single assembly method for both shows, to be tailored to each space. Using standard eighteen-gauge metal framing C-joists and studs, slotted and bolted together with fluorescent lights inside and Mylar film clipped to the outside, we created eight linear light boxes—glowing strips of project images. Each strip contains two metal C-joists or C-studs: one turned outward and containing the images, the other turned inward and containing the title decals. This method also allowed one prototype to be useable for both installations.

The differences in the width of the installed pieces correlate to the various sizes of the exhibited projects. The eight projects fall into five size categories, which then inform the five widths of C-joist and C-stud (four, six, eight, ten, and twelve inches). A four-inch C-stud is thus used for a small project a thousand square feet or less in area and a twelve-inch C-joist is used for a large urban project. The differences in the sites did finally drive the organizational and mounting methodologies of the two shows.

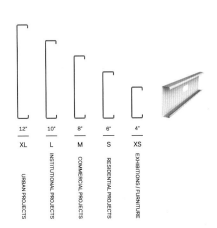
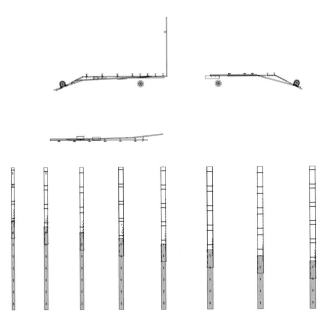

left: Standard C-joist sizes correlating to project sizes
right: Plans
opposite top: Parsons
opposite bottom: UT Austin

## Site Lines: Parsons the New School for Design

Responding to the small size of the space and its location in a public corridor, the installation strategy for this show had two components. The first was to attach the assemblies to the walls in a stacked formation. The second was to bend and extend the "lines" to latch them onto existing columns, run them down adjacent hallways, and have them miss the intervening corners. Vertical mounting, coupled with display articulation, addresses the constant pedestrian traffic in and through the space. In addition, the extension of the pieces into neighboring spaces as they turn corners and move down hallways exposes the undefined boundaries of the gallery. The result is a series of illuminated linear "Site Lines" that display our work and run through and out of the confines of the gallery space.

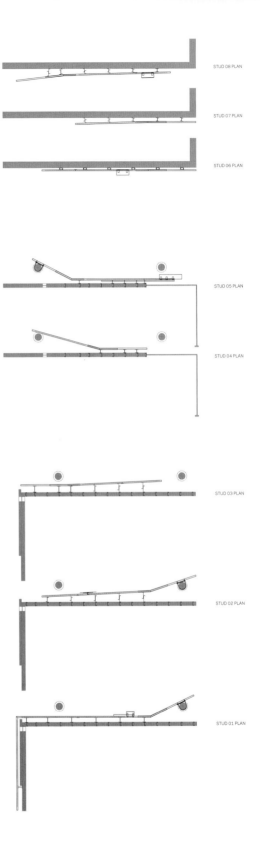

STUD 08 PLAN

STUD 07 PLAN

STUD 06 PLAN

STUD 05 PLAN

STUD 04 PLAN

STUD 03 PLAN

STUD 02 PLAN

STUD 01 PLAN

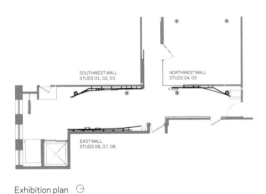

SOUTHWEST WALL
STUDS 01, 02, 03

NORTHWEST WALL
STUDS 04, 05

EAST WALL
STUDS 06, 07, 08

Exhibition plan

**top and right:** Plans of Parsons show
**bottom:** Parsons installation

114

Parsons installation views

## Line Weights: University of Texas at Austin

The gallery space in Austin was very large. Thirty-five feet deep and seventy feet long, it was devoid of obstacles and through traffic. In contrast to Parsons, where the exhibited pieces occupied the perimeter of the space and were mounted to the walls, the Austin display strips hung in the center of the room and filled the space. Visitors to the gallery walked around and among the eight exhibition lines, which were mounted from the ceiling on cables clamped to the existing concrete beams. Each straight line of display was spaced in response to the architectural rhythm of the room (the existing ceiling structure, windows, and entry doors). The width of the C-joists, as in the Parsons show, related to the projects; but for the show in Austin, in which the pieces were hung, the element of gravity also figured into the display assemblage. Smaller projects were presented as "lighter," while larger projects were given more weight, by hanging one end of the strip closer to the floor. The angle of the pieces began as horizontal, as the smallest project and C-joist hovered forty-two inches off the floor, and angled in at four-inch increments, so that the last display line canted from forty-two inches at one end to six inches above the floor at the other, creating a wave through the gallery. The result was a series of illuminated "Line Weights," measured both in dimension and in weight.

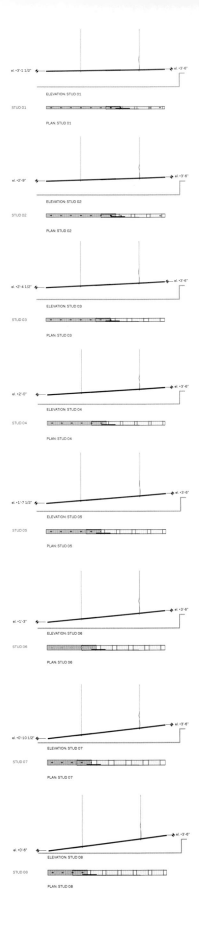

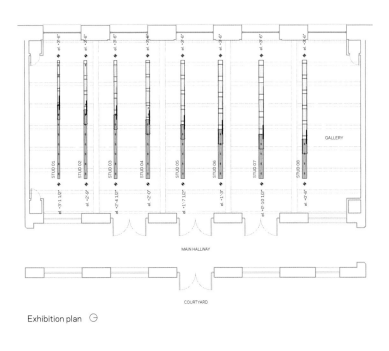

Exhibition plan ⊖

Plans of UT Austin show

UT Austin installation views

# Piranesi as Designer / Cooper-Hewitt, National Design Museum

LOCATION: NEW YORK, NEW YORK / PROGRAM: EXHIBITIONS
ORGANIZATION: STATISTICAL / LOCAL CODE: ART OBJECTS DISPLAYED
AREA: 6,000 SF / COMPLETION DATE: 2007

This exhibition design is for a show that focuses on the designed objects and drawings of the eighteenth-century Italian architect Giovanni Battista Piranesi. The show's inventory describes the scope of Piranesi's work, and part of our idea for the design was to group the collection into several categories and sub-groupings based on time, place, and concept. The show includes, in addition to the original Piranesi pieces, two interactive rooms—one a reading room and the other a room of work by contemporary architects who look toward Piranesi as an influence. Our display cases and platform designs are formulated as methods for explaining these sub-groupings within the larger themes of the show.

Three among the many strong strategies that Piranesi utilized to convey his theories of recombined eclecticism were a stark palette (primarily in his graphic work) of blacks, whites, and grays; a commitment to gesture and movement in various aspects of his artistic and architectural production; and the use of pattern. In the design of this exhibition, therefore, these artistic intentions, which helped to place Piranesi's work in high relief against other philosophical and design trends of the time, are investigated and interpreted for various display and experiential methodologies.

This exhibition design pulls apart the black, white, and gray palette of Piranesi's drawings and etchings to assign a black-and-gray palette to rooms that contain original work and a white palette to interactive rooms, containing work reproduced for this exhibition and current work by other architects. In this way, the palette of the show plays directly off the graphic nature of Piranesi's work, focusing the viewers' attention on the actual pieces presented in this exhibition. Piranesi's flat work and black, white, and gray etchings, as well as his furniture and designed objects in gold, silver, and vibrant material colors, stand out against the muted background. The two white interactive rooms occur between the black-and-gray original-work rooms, creating a break in the flow of the exhibition, or an interval where the actual architecture and designed objects are not the primary focus, so that another part of Piranesi's story can be told by the exhibition curators.

Piranesi's predisposition toward gesture and movement were also informative to the design of the show. The story of Piranesi's development, multivalent interests, research, and influences required a spatial attention and a breakdown of the larger spaces of the museum. Gesture and movement configure places of pause and focus, which allow the exhibition to be considered both as a whole and as constituent parts. In this regard, the gestural casework is designed in two distinct ways: as a vertical apparatus and as a horizontal platform. The first two rooms contain mostly flat work and books, so a modular system of plywood panels and steel-tube supports was devised for the vertical flat-work-display panels. These assemblies include bottom rails for didactic texts; top valence flaps that frame and enhance a singular experience with the artwork; and connector pieces of four distinct angles to make the various layouts. For the large middle room, containing furniture and designed objects, a second method of display is used. Built into the walls of the large room, this predominantly horizontal system employs unique gestural forms to create sub-groupings. These platforms shoot out from the walls and into the middle of the space to display pieces of furniture, then recede back toward the wall to allow a close viewing of the surrounding wall-mounted flat work that explains the design of the object pieces.

Overlaid in graphic black onto the gesture panels and casework is a series of gray patterns. The application of these patterns, derived from ancient sources and "new" architectures by Piranesi, is transformed and utilized as a navigational tool to visually link related objects that have been placed together in a group. These patterns are extracted directly from Piranesi's etchings and applied to the casework in the same spirit that Piranesi himself sampled etchings of Etruscan tombs and applied them to his architecture, especially in the facade of the Church of Santa Maria del Priorato.

top: Black and white display method diagram
bottom: Plan of exhibition

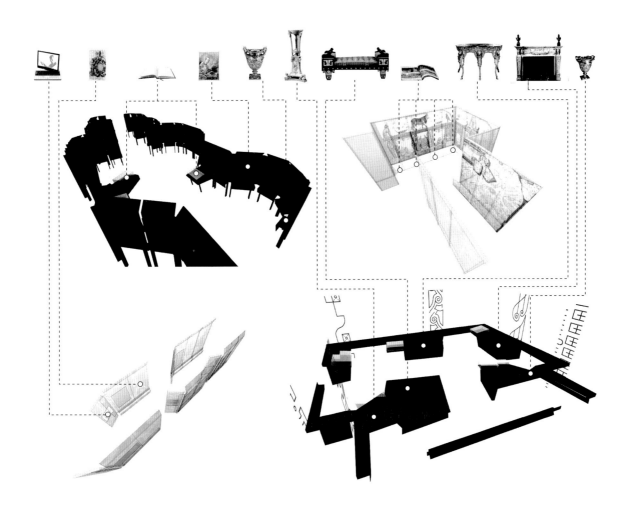

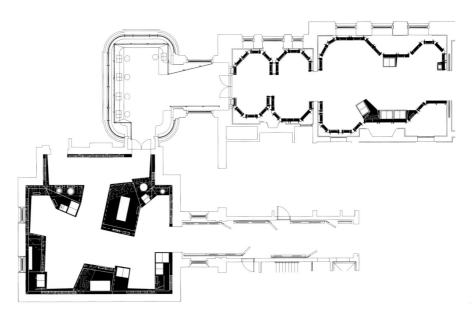

**top:** Pulled-apart diagram, left to right: panel-connector piece, vertical supports, black display panel with original artwork, text, and pattern, patterns sampled from Piranesi etchings
**bottom:** Sections through panels, display cases, and platforms

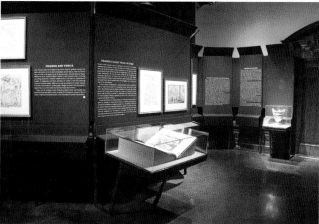

Exhibition rooms with vertical display panels for flat work and books

**top:** Pulled-apart diagram, left to right: black display platform and acrylic display boxes with original Piranesi books, original furniture piece, patterns sampled from Piranesi etchings, Piranesi etchings sampled from Etruscan tombs
**left and middle right:** Exhibition room with horizontal display platforms for large objects and books
**bottom right:** White exhibition room with vertical display panels for flat work and video

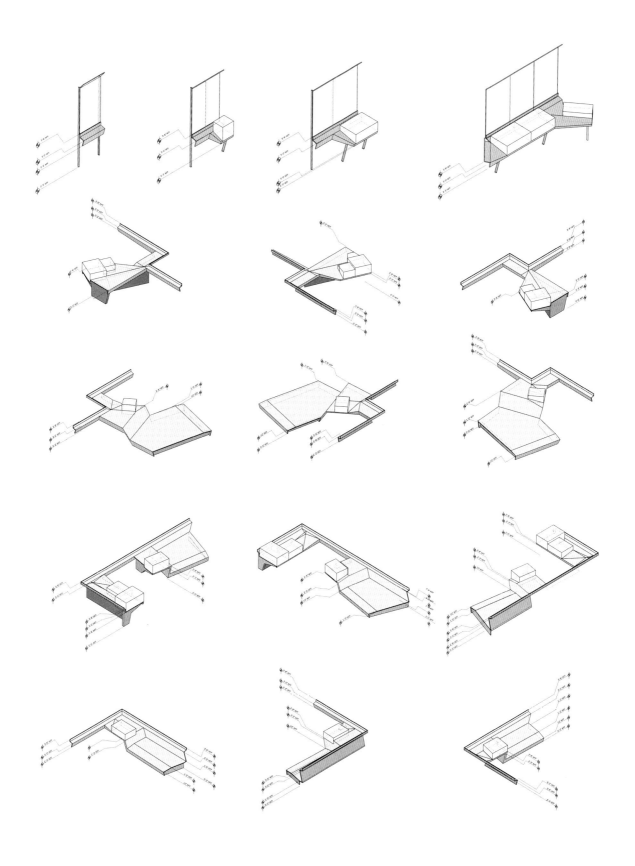

Isometric drawings of vertical and horizontal display panels and platforms

# Frederic Church, Winslow Homer, and Thomas Moran: Tourism and the American Landscape / Cooper-Hewitt, National Design Museum

LOCATION: NEW YORK, NEW YORK / PROGRAM: EXHIBITIONS / ORGANIZATION: STATISTICAL / LOCAL CODE: ART OBJECTS DISPLAYED
AREA: 12,000 SF / COMPLETION DATE: 2006

This project is an exhibition design for a show of nineteenth-century American landscape paintings, drawings, prints, and objects. The show's intent is to demonstrate the relationship between "studies" and "finished" works of art from the late nineteenth century as they related to a then-burgeoning tourist industry. The exhibition presents the work of three master artists who depicted various regions of the country that were opening up to tourism at the time. The collection is loosely grouped in two categories: masterworks and ephemera. The masterworks consist of finished paintings and drawings; the ephemera consist of postcards and other travel-related objects that were used to promote tourism. The ephemera are works by the three master artists, as well as by lesser-known contemporary commercial artists. While reviewing the group-ings, we learned that many so-called "low," or commercial, artworks in the show were studies for the "high-art" paintings. This fact and the larger connections that the exhibition posits between artworks and the tourism industry informed our design of the show, whose primary goal is to facilitate a connection between the two types of artwork.

Two methods of display are therefore used in relation to the two groups. The masterworks are hung on the walls at the perimeter of the rooms of the Carnegie mansion that houses the museum. These works are spaced apart from one another and from the ephemera, so that they can be viewed independently, as in a typical museum show. The ephemera, by contrast, occupy the center of each room and are housed in transparent acrylic cases, with billboard sides made of the same material attached to the cases. The transparency of these display cases allows these commercial art pieces to be viewed in conjunction with the masterworks that are visible

on the surrounding walls. Additionally, the backs of flat work can be viewed by walking around the billboard pieces, thereby heightening the sense of multiple readings among the works throughout the show.

These various methods of display function to narrow the gap between "high" and "low" artworks in the show and to explain that they are both, in many ways, part of a single marketing system. This tourism industry's goal was to sell an image—an ideal of an undisturbed natural America—to late-nineteenth-century travelers and to use whatever visual media was available at the time to do so.

Two other visual technologies are used in the exhibition: stereophotography and film. Stereophotography, a three-dimensional photography technique developed in the nine-teenth century, was used widely to produce souvenir objects, much the way the popular View-Master cards were used in the early- to mid-twentieth century. These cards contained images of tourist attractions. For this show, we created a stereo viewing environment, a room where the visitor is confronted with a wall-size double image of a landscape photo. Here, the visitor can see various stereo cards through a twenty-first-century computer viewer that uses the same doubling tech-nique to create a three-dimensional image. At the entry to the exhibition, starting at the base of the stairwell and traveling up to the second floor, the visitor confronts a twenty-three-foot-high film projection of an early Thomas Edison film of Niagara. Like the ephemera, the moving image is an advertise-ment, or invitation, to see the exhibition on the upper level of the museum. The design of these two environments rounds out the explanation of the visual means employed by the tourism industry at the time.

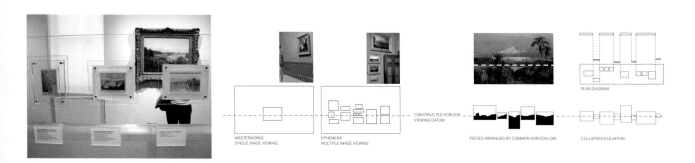

left: Transparency view through "low" to "high" art objects
right: Viewing-methodology-relationship diagram

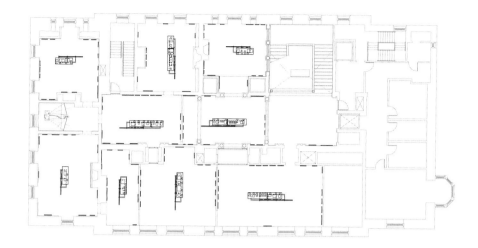

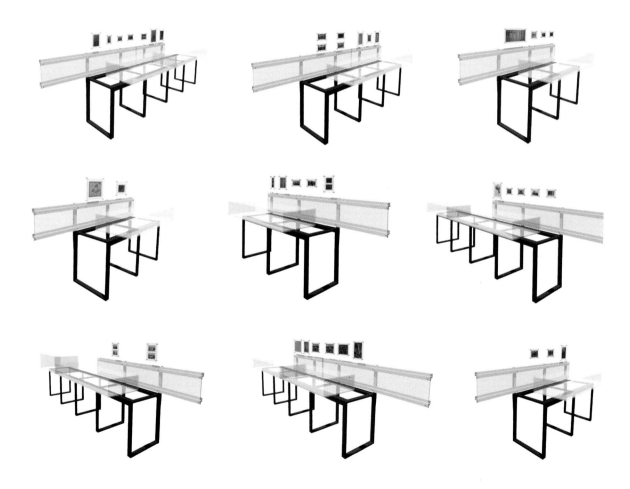

**top:** Plan of exhibition space
**bottom:** Rendered view of nine display cases

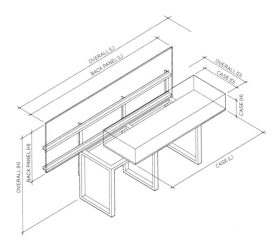

**top:** Views of the display cases and exhibition space
**bottom left:** Isometric, typical display case components

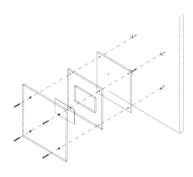 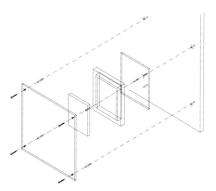 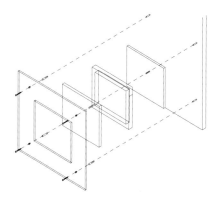

top: Transparent panel details
bottom: Mounting display method for ephemera at transparent back panel

**CITY**

# Filter Parking

LOCATION: ANYWHERE NEEDED / PROGRAM: AUTOMATED PARKING LOT AND ASSOCIATED PROGRAMS
ORGANIZATION: STATISTICAL / LOCAL CODE: PARKING
AREA: VARIABLE / COMPLETION DATE: THE NEAR FUTURE

Filter Parking confronts the negative impact of parking-lot sprawl in cities and suburbs; along freeways; around malls, shopping centers, and sports arenas; in downtown areas; at airports; and at any other car- and people-intensive environment. American cities and suburbs are inundated with seas of cars, which are housed in unconsidered and wasteful structures and on asphalt expanses. This research explores the morphology of the American parking lot and posits new configurations for parking cars and providing space for people. Filter Parking addresses major issues of land use, air pollution, and stormwater runoff, as well as issues of responsible and creative material usage that conventional parking lots ignore in cities, suburbs, and along highways. In addition, Filter Parking illuminates the political and financial issues associated with parking lots and garages in urban situations.

Our interest in creating a hybridized typology centered around the parking lot, in integrating public and green programs, and in latching onto existing infrastructures grew out of a 2003 competition to design one such facility in Chicago. The site of the competition was paradigmatic of several specifically American car-intensive conditions, which we have gone on to address in Filter Parking. First, the Kennedy Expressway, which runs underneath the competition site, was built under the auspices of the Eisenhower Highway Act of 1956; it represents a classic worn-out monocultural infrastructure. Second, the urban parking garage, which is fat with concrete and destroys the street, is in great evidence, as a base for three tall towers, right next door to the site. Third, services for those who don't drive cars was left unconsidered when the 1956 Highway Act provided for fast wide roads to move people and military equipment at extreme speeds across the country. (What to do without the Cold War Soviet enemy?) And the lack of green as a carbon offset was sorely in evidence at its location adjacent to the highway and around the neighboring parking garages.

In Filter Parking, we seek out infrastructures in need of renewal and complexity for possible sites of implementation. With oil on the wane and regime change close at hand in America, other modes of transport with other modes of propulsion are fast approaching. Witness grassroots developments in technologies for bicycles, motorcycles, and alternately fueled cars. Filter Park provides for fueling and storage of these new transportation forms and uses automated parking technology to move cars, reduce emissions, and take up less land for parking. It also integrates trees and other plantings to clean the air and embed the park program in this new typology. The equation for this project is simple:

**Automated Parking + Trees + Architecture = Filter Parking**
Automated parking comprises various methods of storing cars off the street and is widely used in Asia and Europe, where the technology is tried-and-true. Computer-driven, fast, efficient, and clean, this type of parking system is based on materials-handling technologies that move objects of specific sizes or containers on x-y-z axes into storage slots. The materials are then returned to the user when recalled through a computer program. Warehouses and libraries utilize such technologies. In automated parking systems, various forms are in use and others are in development: straight runs along central tracks with cars slotted, tail in, one or two deep, run on motorized palettes and vertical chain-drives; the same straight configuration serves as a glorified forklift; baskets rotate on a belt drive; and various radial configurations are arranged in a single circle or concentrically. These are just some of the forms that automated parking takes.

Since we always add a park program to this multifaceted typology, we have researched various tree species that are particularly robust in urban and high-exhaust conditions. Additionally, because our park inhabits a nontraditional ground condition, tough city trees with low root systems and a resiliency to wind are required.

opposite: Parking-lot land-use diagram

### Commuter Rail Station

 CONVENTIONAL PARKING
Poor use of land and waterfront, as well as long walk for pedestrians.

PROPOSED AUTOMATED PARKING
Bar Structure.
Commuters can easily access the parking structure from the train platforms.

LAND SAVED - PROPOSED GREEN SPACE

### Stadium

CONVENTIONAL PARKING
Creates sprawl, poor land use, long walk for pedestrians. Land remains empty when no event is occurring.

PROPOSED AUTOMATED PARKING
Crescent Structure.
Easier access for fans arriving and leaving. Structure can incorporate signage and scoreboard.

LAND SAVED - PROPOSED GREEN SPACE

### Airport

CONVENTIONAL PARKING
Parking and rental car companies are inaccessible from terminal.

 PROPOSED AUTOMATED PARKING
Bridge Structure.
Parking is accessible from all points as well as functions as a bridge connecting terminals.

LAND SAVED - PROPOSED GREEN SPACE

### Pier

CONVENTIONAL PARKING
Approximately 50% of cars driving in downtown areas are looking for parking.

PROPOSED AUTOMATED PARKING
Linear Structure.
Reduction in carbon monoxide exhaust and traffic congestion in and around city.

### Mall

CONVENTIONAL PARKING
Considerable amounts of land taken up for parking.

PROPOSED AUTOMATED PARKING
Parasite Structure.
Shoppers do not have to walk far distances to get to car.

LAND SAVED - PROPOSED GREEN SPACE

### Highway Interchange

CONVENTIONAL PARKING
Creates more sprawl, poor use of land in and around highway turn-abouts.

PROPOSED AUTOMATED PARKING
Ribbon Structure.
Commuters can easily access the parking structure from the existing on-off ramps.

LAND SAVED - PROPOSED GREEN SPACE

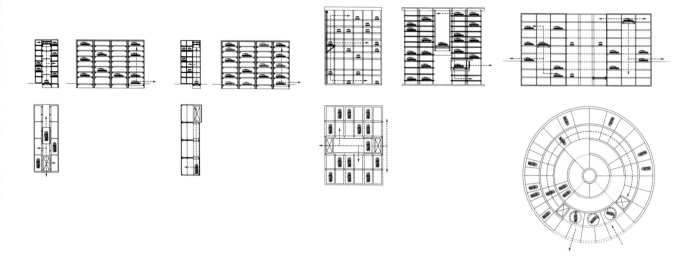

Emissions Analysis for Conventional 924-Space
Parking Garage
- Footprint = 150' x 270'
- Eight levels
- Use of express ramps
- Assuming one turn per day per stall
- Average Vehicle Miles Traveled (VMT) (assuming
  travel to mid-point at fourth level) per car per
  day to park and to exit = 5280' : ( [2 x 240' +
  2 x 90'] x 4 levels) x 2 for entry & exit (assuming
  275 days /year)

Conversion to Pollutants Emitted per Year for an
"Average" Passenger Car and an "Average" Light Truck:
- Hydrocarbons: 3.3 grams / mile = 838,530 grams =
  1,847 lbs. of HC / Y
- Carbon Monoxide: 25.5 grams / mile =
  6,479,550 grams = 7,136 tons of CO / Y
- Nitrogen Oxides: 1.7 grams / mile =
  431,970 grams = 951 lbs. of NOx / Y
- Carbon Dioxide: 1 pound / mile =
  127 tons of $CO_2$ / Y
- Gasoline: .05 gallon / mile =
  12,705 gallons gasoline / Y
- Total average number of vehicle miles traveled in
  conventional garage = 254,100 miles / year

(Traffic and Environment Data from
Robotic Parking, Inc.)

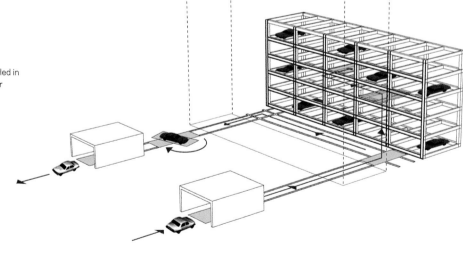

top: Automated-parking-technology configurations
right: Automated-parking operational diagram

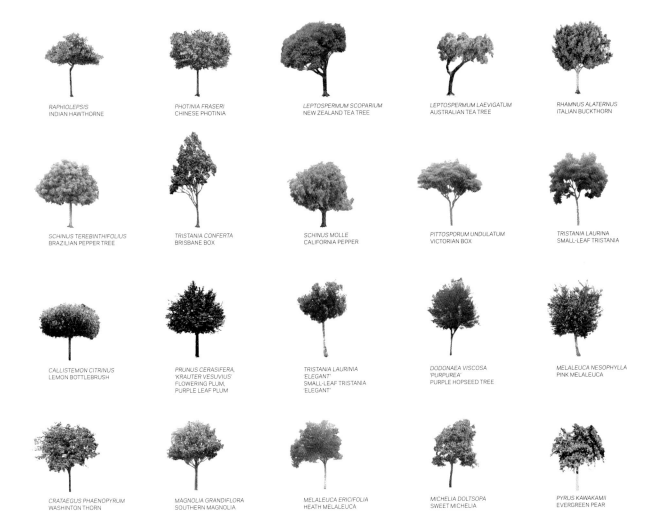

RAPHIOLEPSIS
INDIAN HAWTHORNE

PHOTINIA FRASERI
CHINESE PHOTINIA

LEPTOSPERMUM SCOPARIUM
NEW ZEALAND TEA TREE

LEPTOSPERMUM LAEVIGATUM
AUSTRALIAN TEA TREE

RHAMNUS ALATERNUS
ITALIAN BUCKTHORN

SCHINUS TEREBINTHIFOLIUS
BRAZILIAN PEPPER TREE

TRISTANIA CONFERTA
BRISBANE BOX

SCHINUS MOLLE
CALIFORNIA PEPPER

PITTOSPORUM UNDULATUM
VICTORIAN BOX

TRISTANIA LAURINA
SMALL-LEAF TRISTANIA

CALLISTEMON CITRINUS
LEMON BOTTLEBRUSH

PRUNUS CERASIFERA,
'KRAUTER VESUVIUS'
FLOWERING PLUM,
PURPLE LEAF PLUM

TRISTANIA LAURINIA
'ELEGANT'
SMALL-LEAF TRISTANIA
'ELEGANT'

DODONAEA VISCOSA
'PURPUREA'
PURPLE HOPSEED TREE

MELALEUCA NESOPHYLLA
PINK MELALEUCA

CRATAEGUS PHAENOPYRUM
WASHINTON THORN

MAGNOLIA GRANDIFLORA
SOUTHERN MAGNOLIA

MELALEUCA ERICIFOLIA
HEATH MELALEUCA

MICHELIA DOLTSOPA
SWEET MICHELIA

PYRUS KAWAKAMII
EVERGREEN PEAR

- Trees keep our air supply fresh by absorbing carbon dioxide and producing oxygen.
- In one year, a single tree can absorb as much carbon as is produced by a car driven 26,000 miles.
- Trees lower air temperature by evaporating water in their leaves.
- Trees cut down noise pollution by acting as sound barriers.
- The death of one seventy-year-old tree would return more than three tons of carbon to the atmosphere.
- Trees renew our air supply by absorbing carbon dioxide and producing oxygen.
- Two mature trees can provide enough oxygen for a family of four.
- One tree produces nearly 260 pounds of oxygen each year.
- One acre of trees removes up to 2.6 tons of carbon dioxide each year.

(facts from www.treesaregood.org)

Air-filtering-tree catalog

# Chicago Filter Park

LOCATION: CHICAGO, ILLINOIS / PROGRAM: INFRASTRUCTURAL
ORGANIZATION: STATISTICAL / LOCAL CODE: CARS AND PARKING
AREA: 42,000 SF / COMPETITION DATE: 2003

Chicago Filter Park is the first-place winner of the 2003 Chicago Prize Competition for a thousand-car parking facility. Our proposal begins with three basic strategies: to reconsider the parking facility as part of a larger system of urban infrastructure; to challenge preconceptions of how a parking structure functions, both technologically and environmentally; and to change the way parking lots look.

The site of the competition is an existing empty lot adjacent to the Kennedy Expressway, a paradigm of 1950s American highway construction. We began the competition design by extending the given site to include the area spanning the highway, allowing us to bridge the urban cut of the highway. The location is at the link between the developing west side of Chicago and the downtown Loop, positioning the new parking facility at one of the many key points of crossing on the expressway. Our bridge building sits parallel to the existing Madison Street overpass. Cars occupy the structure above, and buses stop at the terminal building below; but the central open space of the building is for pedestrians and cyclists to cross the expressway free and clear of moving traffic. In this way, the new structure is part of the larger system of transportation infrastructure, which includes not just cars, parking, and buses, but also bikes and pedestrians.

Located on the northern edge of the competition site, the parking facility is composed of two thin linear structures of automated parking (see previous discussion of parking technology in Filter Parking); between them runs a bridge and hanging tree garden, where pedestrians and cyclists can cross the Kennedy Expressway. This non-car access to the parking structure occurs on a series of ramping berms that invert the patterns of the expressway and its strips of highway and ramps. Underneath these pedestrian berms are fans for filtering car exhaust. Automobile access occupies the slices between the berms. The ramping access to the parking garage thus reformulates the morphology of the highway by creating a functioning urban earthwork that provides for pedestrian inhabitation and filtering of automobile exhaust. Cyclists and pedestrians use the ramps as a means of access to and from the building, and a system of fans, filters, and vents cleans the air fouled by the cars waiting to be parked.

Regional park systems around parking lot site from Kennedy Expressway to downtown

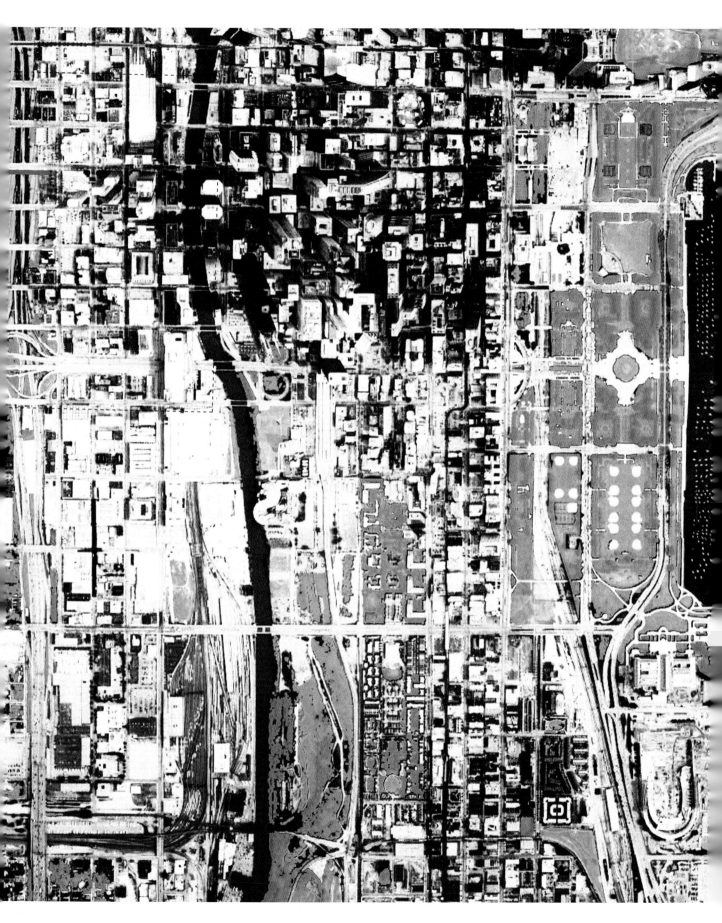

This scheme proposes a two-bar linear automated parking system in order to greatly reduce the physical impact on this urban site of a thousand-car parking structure and its related auto emissions. The elimination of vehicular ramps allows the building to be significantly less massive, just as the elimination of cars' driving in circles in search of parking at rush hour reduces pollution in the building and surrounding area. Moreover, the structural system requires less material and erection time, thereby reducing costs. The net gain in square footage by using this automated system opens up the rest of the site for other green and public programs.

Cars enter the site from the south, drive along the cut-outs of the pedestrian berms, and enter drop-off stations that connect to the main terminal, the bus stop, or the street. Returning to the garage, drivers pick up their cars at pickup stations and exit the building onto Madison Street, on the north side of the structure. All driven automobile traffic stays at the street level, whereas pedestrians and cyclists ramp up to the level above, creating an unobstructed, vehicular-free open plaza.

Promoting the idea that a parking facility can be a public building that includes other amenities, our scheme adds to the competition's program a bus terminal at street level, bike-rental shop, tourist-information office, pedestrian/cyclist bridge at plaza level, and roof-garden cafe that overlooks the skyline from the top level. These additions to the given program expand the concept of an urban parking facility into an intermodal, informational, sustainable public amenity for the city of Chicago.

The layout of the parking is designed to maximize the filtering of light into the central bridge and garden space,

as well as to expose the daily, weekly, and monthly cycle of use. By placing cars against a glass skin, the exterior and interior facades of the two parking structures act as an occupancy sign that changes depending on whether the garage is full or empty. Commuters on the Kennedy Expressway can easily see whether there is plenty of parking space or whether it is full, and pedestrians and cyclists can see the automated parking system in action as they travel on the bridge.

The material of the structure, glass and steel, is used not only as a simple and efficient construction method, but also to foreground the garage as light and luminous—two things not often associated with parking structures. In addition, trees are incorporated into the building not only to act as filtering and cooling devices, but also to reinvent the parking garage as part of a green system for the city. Since there is no ground for planting the trees (the park is sited over the expressway), new sites for an urban landscape are invented. Running parallel along either side of the pedestrian and cyclist bridge is a hovering meadow of sedum planting beds; and above, in the cross bracing of the parking structure, is a hanging tree garden of robust trees with low root systems.

The built-up form of the pedestrian-cyclist entry ramps anchors the light, open structure of the parking building. These berms are made of concrete and wood, like a boardwalk with linear planting beds and benches.

The use of light, finally, is an important part of the scheme. Both natural and artificial light flood the structure. During the day, light passes through the glass facades, mingling with the shadows of the parked cars and hanging trees. In the evening, the structure is a glowing sign of mechanically moving cars, illuminated tree plantings, and a roof-garden cafe.

Highway view of Filter Park garage

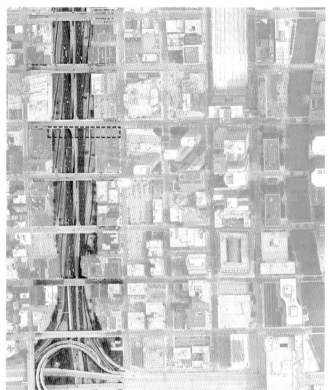

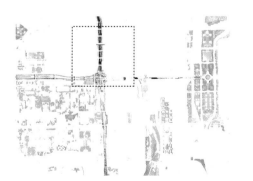

AREA OF SITE

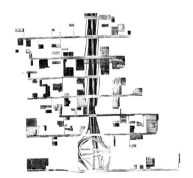

EXISITING PARKING LOTS

PARKING VS. PARK SQ. FOOTAGE
- TOTAL PARKING SQ. FOOTAGE: 1,426,000 SQ. FT.
- TOTAL PARK SQ. FOOTAGE: 72,000 SQ. FT.

**top left:** Aerial site plan at Kennedy Expressway
**top right:** Plan
**bottom, left to right:** Existing park and parking lot
planametric density diagrams

1 Primary auto entry
2 Mechanical auto lift
3 Auto drop-off
4 Bus, taxi, and auto lower
  terminal
5 Bus / taxi stop
6 Toilet
7 Pedestrian / cyclist ramp
8 Plaza area
9 Suspended meadow
10 Car park
11 Bicycle rental /
   storage park
12 Terminal area
13 Information / newsstand
14 Structural cross bracing /
   hanging tree garden
15 Roof cafe
16 Outdoor roof terrace /
   garden

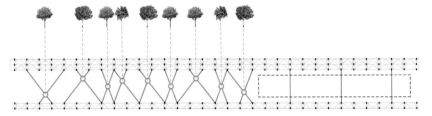

Structural plan

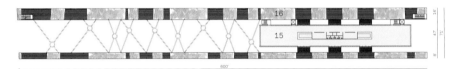

Plan at roof cafe and garden level

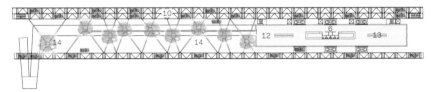

Plan at terminal building level

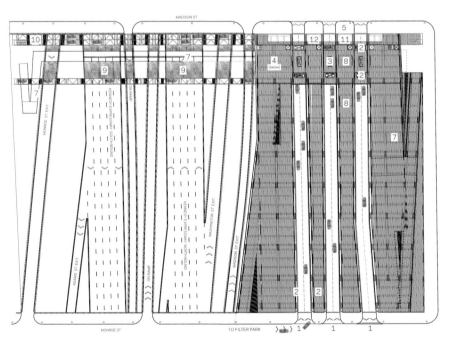

Plan at street level

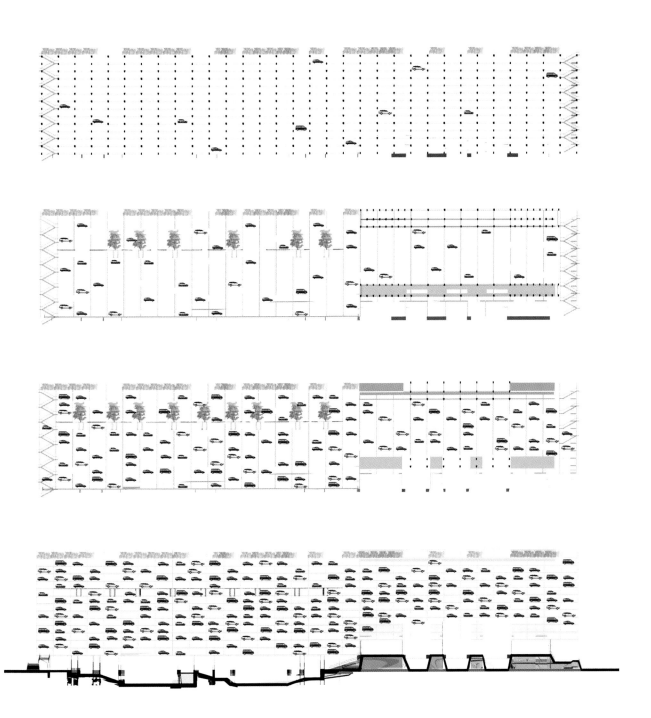

top to bottom: Section / elevation schedule:
three AM, midnight, afternoon rush hour, midday

top: Entry view
bottom: Pedestrian and cyclist upper-plaza view

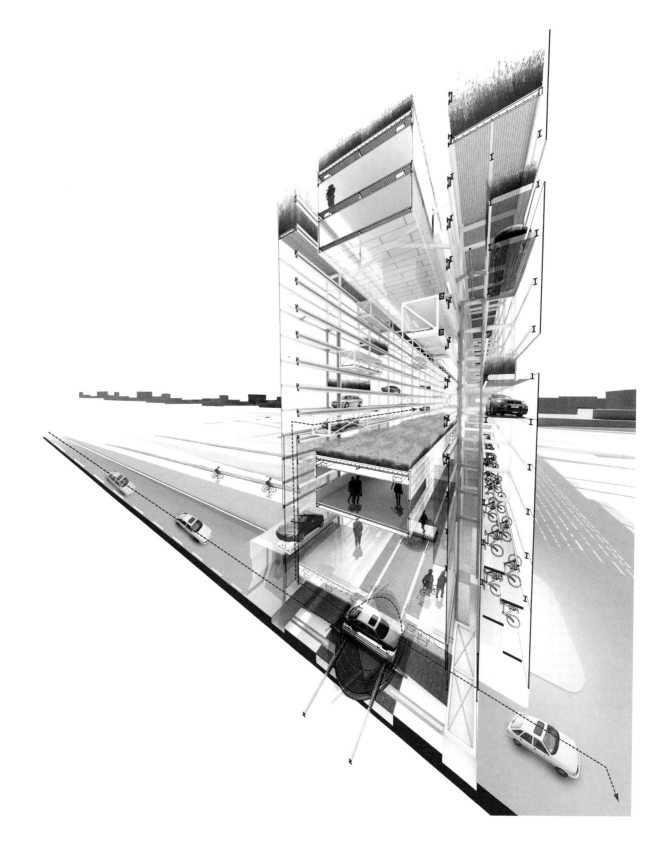

Section perspective cut through automobile entry, automated parking system,
main plaza and bike rental, terminal building, and roof cafe

View below automated parking system from Kennedy Expressway

EXISTING PARKING LOTS
PINK AREAS = PROPOSED AUTOMATED-PARKING PARKING
GREEN AREAS = LAND RECLAIMED, PROPOSED PARK SPACE

PROPOSED GREEN

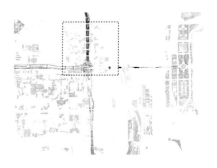

AREA OF SITE WITH PROJECTED GREEN

**top:** Inside automated parking system at hanging tree garden and structural cross bracing
**bottom:** Projected green park and parking lot planametric density diagrams based on pavement to green density transfer

# Greenwich Street Park Apartments

LOCATION: NEW YORK, NEW YORK / PROGRAM: RESIDENTIAL
ORGANIZATION: STATISTICAL / LOCAL CODE: PARKS/PARKING
AREA: 45,000 SF / PROPOSAL DATE: 2004

This project is a proposal for a thirty-five-unit apartment building in lower Manhattan. The developer wanted, in addition to the residential units, commercial space at the street and the rooftop, as well as a revenue-producing parking garage. However, the budget for the project ruled out placing the garage below street level. Moreover, it was important to us that the project include a garden space. With these requirements and desires in mind, we knew that one of the main challenges of the project was going to be how to fit the units, the parking, and the green on the given site.

The design solution began with an investigation of park spaces and parking lots in this area of Manhattan. Our analysis revealed that there is a lot of parking and very few local parks within the tight confines of lower Manhattan. It therefore became even more important to us that the project include a public park, however small. And to satisfy the developer's requirement for revenue-producing parking on the site, an automated parking system is proposed (see a discussion of automated parking in Filter Parking). This parking system is located at the rear of the lot and doubles as a vertical urban trellis. In addition, it is quiet, it saves square footage by eliminating the circling of cars in pursuit of parking spaces, and it reduces the carbon-monoxide exhaust of idling cars. It is also cost-effective, because it provides for the parking above ground and therefore saves the excavation costs of an underground parking facility.

From a design standpoint, the automated system operates at several levels. It is engaging to watch and clean to operate. The steel structure is leveraged to create a vertical urban trellis, or twelve-story garden wall, for the residents of the apartment building. The plants of the trellis cascade down to a rear-yard garden at ground level. The square footage gained is used to create a semipublic pocket park, one that is open during the business hours of the market and cafe below. Finally, a fire stair hangs off the parking structure, providing a second means of egress for the units.

Situated mid-block, the building has two primary facades. The front is a smooth double skin that bends to the zoning requirements for setback, provides an extra layer of protection from sound on the street side, and facilitates the heating and cooling of the building naturally. The rear facade pushes in and out in response to the glass-enclosed kitchens and open balconies of the individual units. In this way, the rear facade is the active facade, since it is more open and engages the vertical garden and park below.

All units are designed as floor-through duplexes in a skip-stop configuration. This is beneficial for two reasons. It is a highly efficient layout that maximizes the square footage allotted to each unit, and it ensures that each unit has a space (or two) facing the rear vertical garden. The building also takes advantage of the zoning law's provision for extra floors to accommodate a health-club facility by proposing a luxury spa at the top of the building.

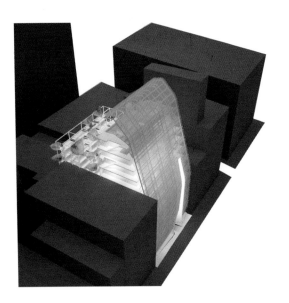

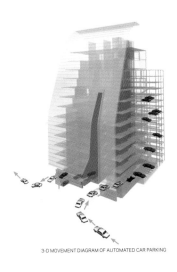

3-D MOVEMENT DIAGRAM OF AUTOMATED CAR PARKING

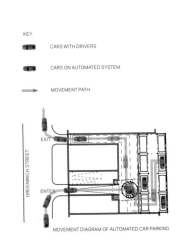

KEY

CARS WITH DRIVERS

CARS ON AUTOMATED SYSTEM

MOVEMENT PATH

MOVEMENT DIAGRAM OF AUTOMATED CAR PARKING

**left:** Building view in context
**right:** Parking system diagram: Three-dimensional movement diagram of automated car parking, Plan diagram of automated car parking

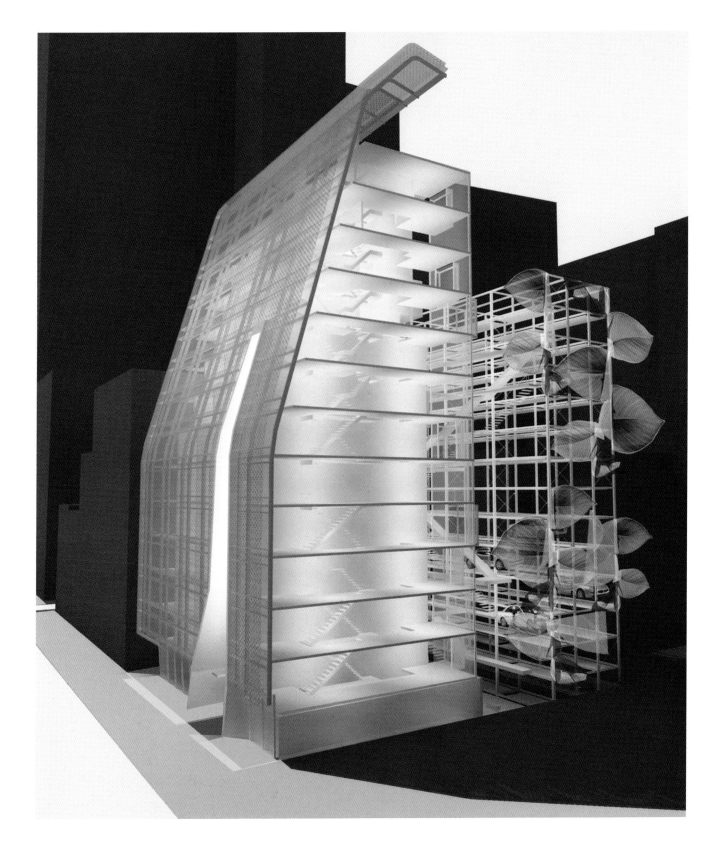

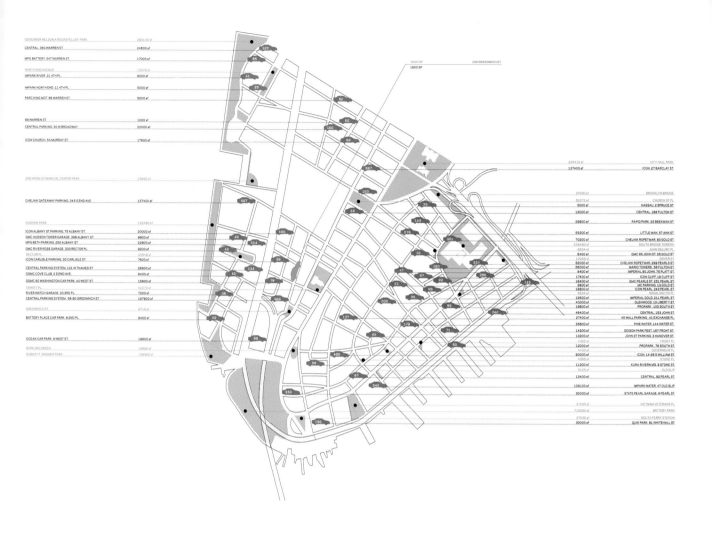

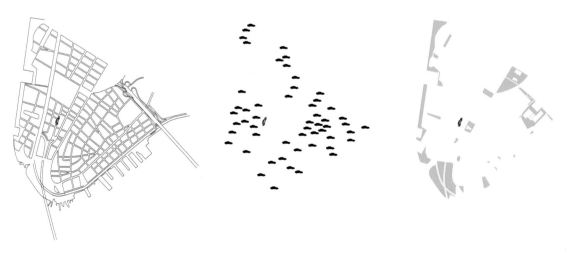

**top:** Lower Manhattan park and parking-lot diagram
**bottom, left to right:** Street grid, Parking lots, Parks

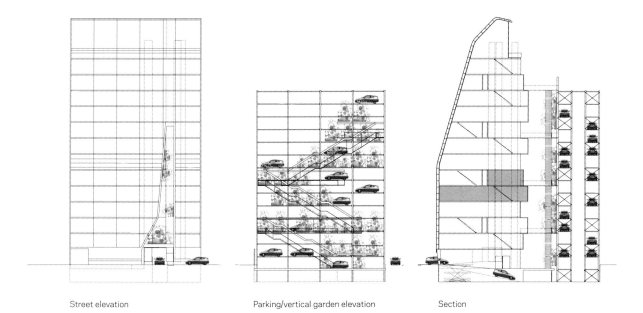

Street elevation          Parking/vertical garden elevation          Section

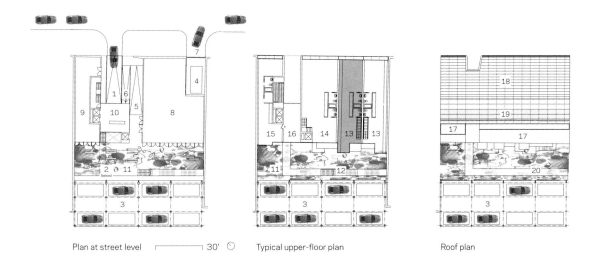

Plan at street level  ⌐────────┐ 30' ↻          Typical upper-floor plan          Roof plan

1   Entry ramp down to parking system          11   Garden
2   Parking system turnaround                  12   Fire stair
3   Parking system                             13   1-Bedroom duplex apt.
4   Exit lift to street                        14   2-Bedroom duplex apt.
5   Entry ramp down to market/store            15   1-Bedroom single-story apt.
6   Entry ramp up to residence lobby           16   Elevator mezzanine
7   Exit at street level                       17   Roof terrance
8   Market/commercial space                    18   Double-glazed curtain wall
9   Commercial space                           19   Photovoltaic panels at roof glass
10  Residence lobby                            20   Second-egress park hallway

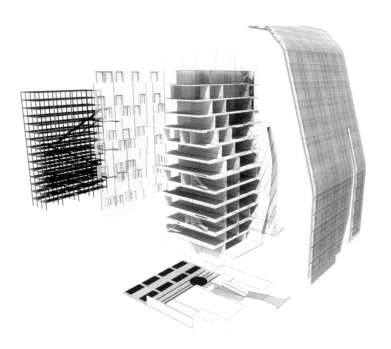

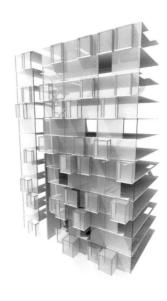

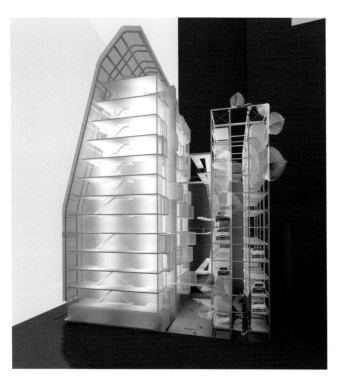

**top left:** Rendered view of building components pulled apart;
(left to right) automated parking structure, glass facade, apartments, circulation core,
front glass and mesh facade; (bottom) lower-level parking entry
**top right:** Rear-yard glass facades
**bottom left:** Rear vertical garden and parking system view
**bottom right:** Automated parking and garden trellis view

Street facade with sliver view into rear garden

# Spaces Between the Hills

LOCATION: RAMALLAH-JERUSALEM-BETHLEHEM, ISRAEL / PROGRAM: INFRASTRUCTURAL
ORGANIZATION: SYNTACTIC / LOCAL CODE: VALLEY SYSTEMS
COMPLETION DATE: 2000 / IN COLLABORATION WITH DAVID SNYDER

This project is a theoretical urban-design proposal for the greater region of Ramallah-Jerusalem-Bethlehem that was initially published in a book called *The Next Jerusalem*, edited by Michael Sorkin. It is the outcome of selective observations of the physical conditions and daily activities of the Ramallah-Jerusalem-Bethlehem region, though by no means do these observations constitute an exhaustive study of the region's complex interplay of political, social, cultural, and religious elements.

The project begins with two investigations: the first examines the natural topography of the region and how that topography affects urban growth; the second charts the schedule of daily life and how that schedule calibrates the particular temporal rhythm of the region.

The topographic analysis shows that the Ramallah-Jerusalem-Bethlehem region is profoundly shaped by two unique valley systems, one entering from the east and the other from the west, which extrude the region into a

north-south linear urban formation. These natural valleys, or "spaces between the hills," have functioned as the true physical borders in the region and are the sites for our proposed interventions.

As natural conditions of the landscape determine the built environment in the region, so does the confluence of the Christian, Muslim, and Jewish prayer times—representing the annual sacred cycle—frame the structure of daily life. The communities' activity occurs in the intervals between prayer. Therefore, because the sacred schedules of the three major religions in the area are not synchronous and because the various religious communities share the same regional space, there are overlaps and gaps where the cycle of one faith impacts the daily activities of the others. The temporal structure of the region is given largely by the staccato of daily, weekly, monthly, and yearly prayer times.

Our proposal consists of a series of suspended structures between two nodes (hills). The sites offer new territories for

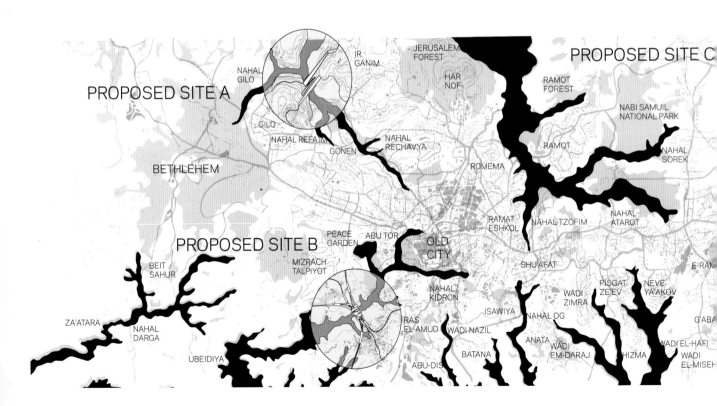

Composite plan of three proposed sites

building within a historically and culturally "closed system."
By choosing this place as the locus of our intervention toward
future development within the region, we hope to demonstrate
a vision of the region as an integrated whole whose upper-
most layer is founded, not on the disputed earth, but on those
interstices which have traditionally acted as natural boundaries
and defining edges, separating neighborhoods and
communities.

The proposal is for three sites. Each site consists of a
spanning structure that includes residential, commercial,
educational, recreational, and municipal elements, along with
a central regional programmatic function. Individually and as
a group, they become part of a larger network of infrastructural
bridges that connect existing adjacent, but separate, communities. Similar to one another as spanning structures, the bridges
employ different architectural strategies in relation to the
different topographic conditions they cross.

Site A

Site B

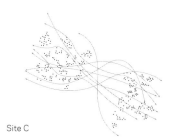

Site C

**right:** Connection and flow diagrams of the three proposed sites

## Proposed Site A: Recreational Seesaw

This spanning structure is conceived of as a seesaw that negotiates the topography with a series of ramps. The central regional programmatic function for this site is a recreational node composed of a ramping park system that generates the primary form of this typology. In this space between the hills, playing fields exist and shape the connection to the existing adjacent neighborhoods of Ir Ganim and Gilo, as well as to the Refa'im and Nahal Gilo nature preserves.

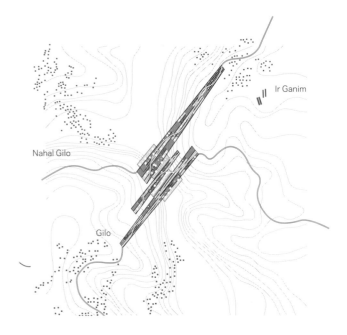

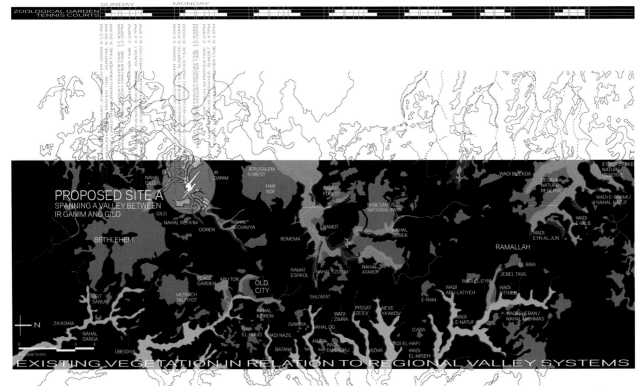

top: Proposed site A site plan
bottom: Proposed site A regional plan

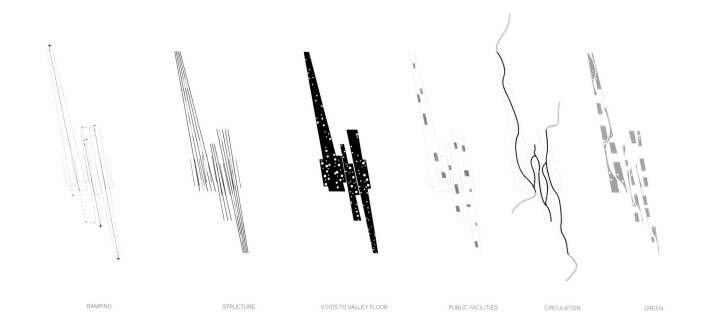

RAMPING  STRUCTURE  VOIDS TO VALLEY FLOOR  PUBLIC FACILITIES  CIRCULATION  GREEN

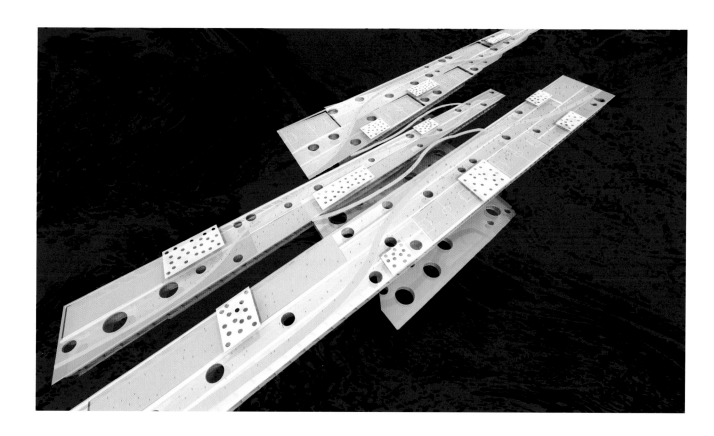

top: Ramping park system, component diagrams
bottom: Park system, aerial view

## Proposed Site B: Municipal Necklace

This spanning structure is seen as a necklace that stretches across the hills and suspends beaded structures. The central regional programmatic function for this site is a bureaucratic/municipal center composed of a series of buildings threaded along a major new east-west regional artery. In this space between the hills, city offices and the regional government complex exist and form the connection to the adjacent existing neighborhoods of Abu-Dis and Mizrach Talpiyot; they also establish a visual connection both to and from the historic core of the Old City.

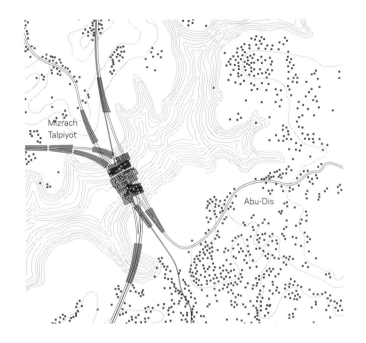

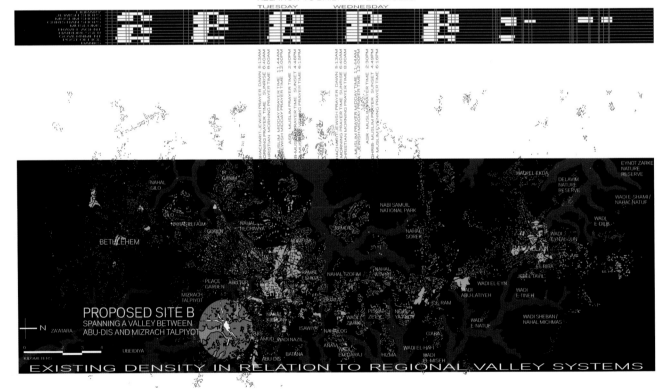

top: Proposed site B site plan
bottom: Proposed site B regional plan

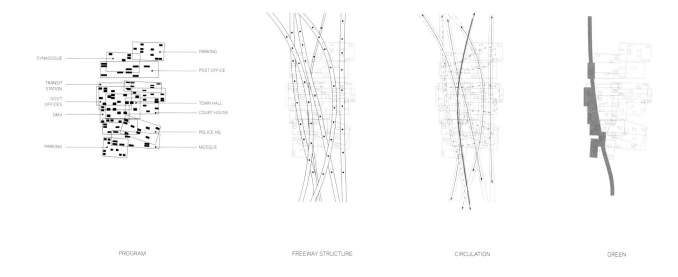

PROGRAM          FREEWAY STRUCTURE          CIRCULATION          GREEN

SYNAGOGUE — PARKING

— POST OFFICE

TRANSIT STATION

GOV'T OFFICES — TOWN HALL

DMV — COURT HOUSE

— POLICE HQ

PARKING — MOSQUE

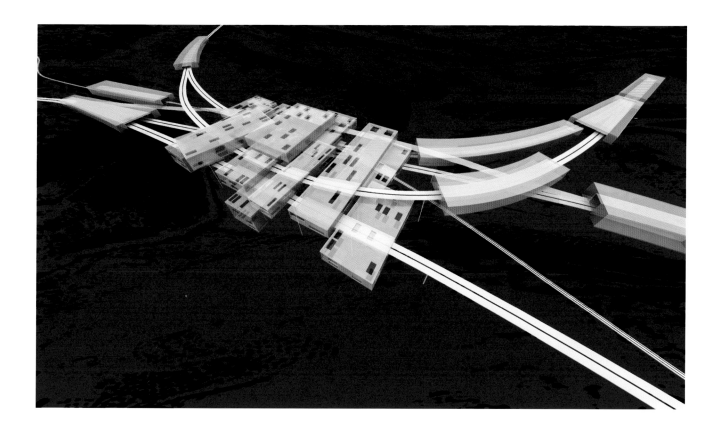

**top:** Municipal necklace component diagrams
**bottom:** Aerial view

## Proposed Site C: Transportation Staple

This spanning structure is like a staple that joins the land on either side with a single bar. The central regional programmatic function of this site is a new transportation hub composed of a multilayered, multifunctional terminal for all circulation systems. In this space between the hills, a train, bus, and vehicular interchange exists and forms the connection to the existing adjacent neighborhoods of Beitunya and Givat Ze'ev while creating a western gateway into the newly conceived region.

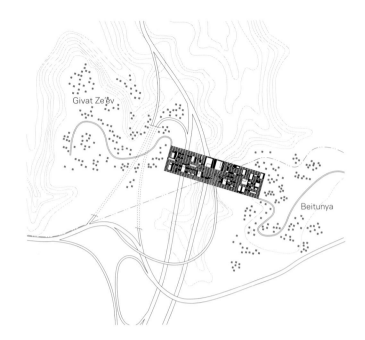

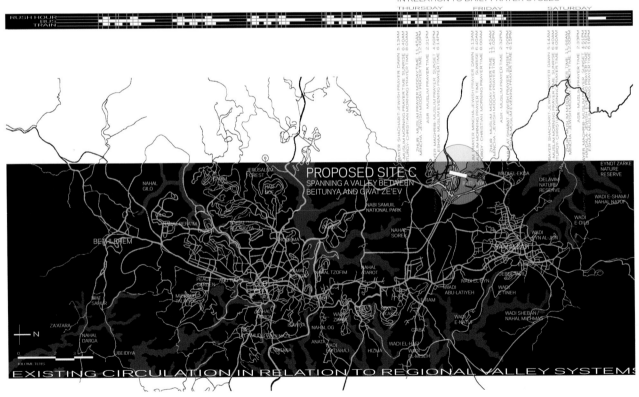

top: Proposed site C site plan
bottom: Proposed site C regional plan

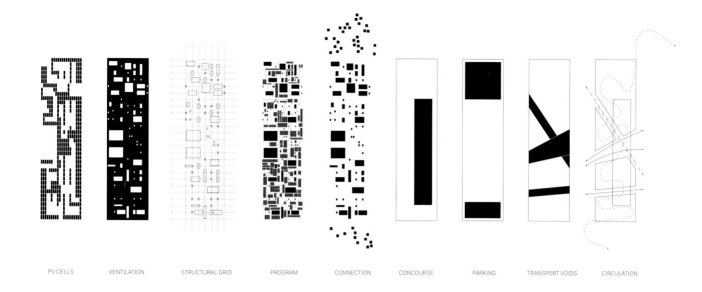

PV CELLS   VENTILATION   STRUCTURAL GRID   PROGRAM   CONNECTION   CONCOURSE   PARKING   TRANSPORT VOIDS   CIRCULATION

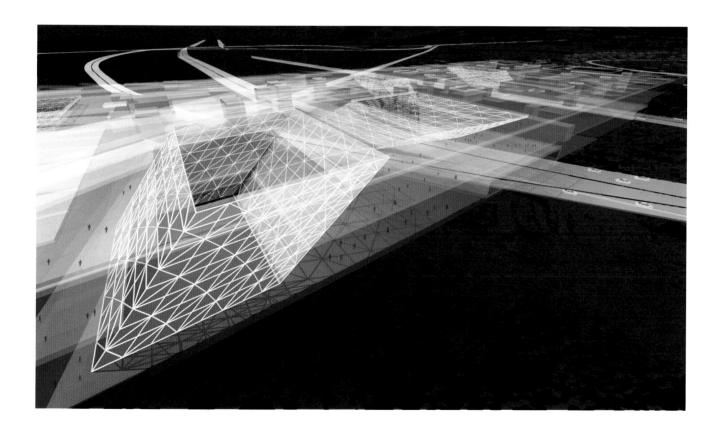

top. Transportation staple, component diagrams
bottom: Aerial view

# Wetland City: New Orleans East Urban Proposal

LOCATION: NEW ORLEANS EAST, LOUISIANA / PROGRAM: INFRASTRUCTURAL
ORGANIZATION: SYNTACTIC / LOCAL CODE: NATURAL AND ARTIFICIAL HIGH POINTS
COMPLETION DATE: 2007

Wetland City is a proposal for a new kind of Gulf Coast urbanism, one that embodies the logic of high-ground habitation and is sustained by reinvigorated natural processes. This project is located in New Orleans, where the soft ground that the city stands on is receding at an alarming rate. Coastal Louisiana has lost an average of thirty-four square miles of land per year for the last fifty years; roughly nineteen hundred square miles. It is projected that by the year 2050 another seven hundred square miles of coastline will disappear.

In the Flooded City of post-Katrina New Orleans, high points and high lines are revealed by the rising waters that inundated the lowlands. An understanding of high and low, how to remove water, and where to go when the flood comes is critical to planning the response to Flooded City, and Wetland City is our response. It constructs and protects wetlands, occupies various types of high ground, and builds new elevated surfaces for sensible habitation. The Wetland City site proposed here is for New Orleans East; one of the severely flooded Katrina sites, it is endangered by the region's rising waters and subsiding land. Water levels are expected to rise by three to six feet in the next hundred years, while the ground is sinking by about two inches per year. As if this slow demise weren't bad enough, storm surges from Katrina delivered the shock that turned the area—previously home to almost a hundred thousand people—into a ghost town. In most of the residential neighborhoods of New Orleans East, the storm water settled at about twelve feet and the surge itself topped twenty feet, sending a primarily lower- and middle-class African American community into the great Katrina Diaspora.

This community's mid- to late-twentieth-century building stock is constructed on slab-on-grade foundations that require mud to be pumped underneath to replace the ground that is subsiding under the sinking houses. Undeniably, the neighborhoods in New Orleans East are constructed insufficiently for their location; and, given the rising waters and soft ground, the present site is itself not sustainable. To address this indefensible current state, Wetland City proposes a phased intervention that installs critical wetland infrastructures and communities by 2025 while supporting the rescue and transit needs of the existing communities during the time when the neighborhoods are still habitable. The time spans of this proposal's phases are 2005—the flood, 2010–2025—the infrastructural response, 2025–2050—only high ground inhabitable, and then in 2105—Wetland City celebrates one hundred years without flood devastation.

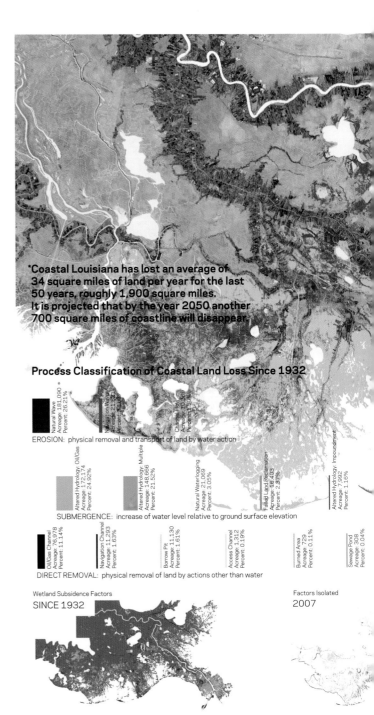

*Coastal Louisiana has lost an average of 34 square miles of land per year for the last 50 years, roughly 1,900 square miles. It is projected that by the year 2050 another 700 square miles of coastline will disappear.*

**Process Classification of Coastal Land Loss Since 1932**

Natural Wave
Acreage: 181,090
Percent: 26.21%

Navigation Channel
Percent: 1.9%

Channel: 13.9%

EROSION: physical removal and transport of land by water action

Altered Hydrology: Oil/Gas
Acreage: 172,174
Percent: 24.92%

Altered Hydrology: Multiple
Acreage: 148,666
Percent: 21.52%

Natural Waterlogging
Acreage: 21,069
Percent: 3.05%

Failed Land Reclamation
Acreage: 16,403
Percent: 2.37%

Altered Hydrology: Impoundment
Acreage: 7,992
Percent: 1.16%

SUBMERGENCE: increase of water level relative to ground surface elevation

Oil/Gas Channel
Acreage: 76,978
Percent: 11.14%

Navigation Channel
Acreage: 11,293
Percent: 1.63%

Borrow Pit
Acreage: 11,130
Percent: 1.61%

Access Channel
Acreage: 1,312
Percent: 0.19%

Burned Area
Acreage: 729
Percent: 0.11%

Sewage Pond
Acreage: 308
Percent: 0.04%

DIRECT REMOVAL: physical removal of land by actions other than water

Wetland Subsidence Factors
SINCE 1932

Factors Isolated
2007

Coastal land loss map and data (Map and Data Source: US Department of the Interior USGS Land Change Analysis; Southeast Louisiana Land Loss, December, 2004.)

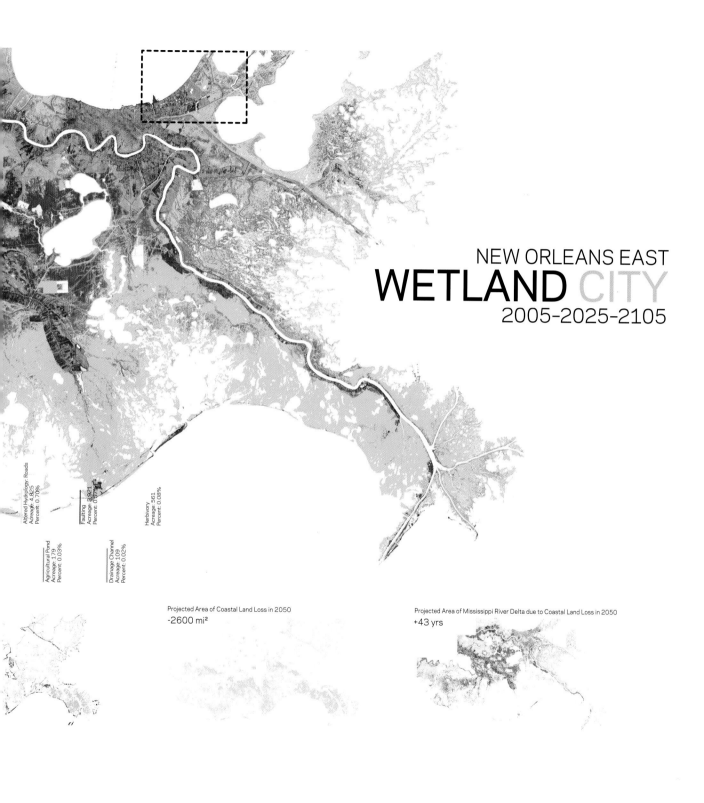

NEW ORLEANS EAST
# WETLAND CITY
## 2005-2025-2105

Altered Hydrology: Roads
Acreage: 4,825
Percent: 0.70%

Faulting
Acreage: 3,921
Percent: 0.57%

Herbivory
Acreage: 561
Percent: 0.08%

Agricultural Pond
Acreage: 179
Percent: 0.03%

Drainage Channel
Acreage: 109
Percent: 0.02%

Projected Area of Coastal Land Loss in 2050
-2600 mi²

Projected Area of Mississippi River Delta due to Coastal Land Loss in 2050
+43 yrs

In the first phase of this proposal, clean, green transit systems, with terminals that double as rescue stations, are strung along an existing east-west corridor, called Chef Menteur Highway. This conduit to Mississippi's suburbs and the rest of the Gulf Coast was formalized in the 1930s under the Huey Long administration and runs from Texas through New Orleans to Florida. It was built on the Gentilly Ridge, a natural high ground formed by a distributary of the Mississippi River that broke off from a hairpin turn just west of New Orleans about five thousand years ago. Critical to the survival of existing neighborhoods during the first phase is the construction along the I-10 highway of rescue-tower stations that contain multiple programs, such as water collection and markets that serve the storm and noncrisis needs of the existing community. The I-10 was built in the 1950s and 1960s as part of the Eisenhower highway program and crosses the country from California to Florida. Its overpasses throughout New Orleans provide artificial high ground that is recommissioned for the above-mentioned crisis and non-flood uses. In the early phases of Wetland City, infrastructures for storm-resistant neighborhoods and housing are built on the lessons learned from existing natural and built high grounds. Most

important—and true to the name of the project—the implementation of a comprehensive wetland-protection plan produces, preserves, and studies wetlands for New Orleans, the Gulf of Mexico region, and any community or region that is endangered by rising global waters.

Additionally, this proposal presupposes that the idiotic Mississippi River Gulf Outlet (MRGO) be filled in and refashioned for a positive use. This seventy-six-mile-long shortcut for shipping from the Gulf to New Orleans's inner harbor runs the length of New Orleans East's southern edge and has the unfortunate consequence of sending storm surges directly at the city and communities along its path. Built from 1956 to 1965, MRGO is a seriously corrosive factor in wetland aquaculture. Its closure was proposed by the Army Corps of Engineers in May 2007, and its future is pending before Congress. It is a major lowland element that in our proposal is reformulated as a high-ground park system. Linear, productive, and punctuated with crisis-management facilities, we propose to rename the area MRGONE Park (MRGO New Orleans East), a scenic corridor for biking and hiking into the Mississippi Delta, as well as a rescue conduit for St. Bernard Parish and New Orleans East.

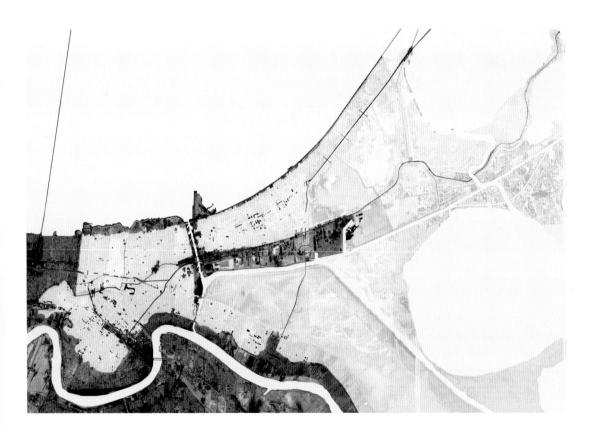

Flooded City, 2005: extent of flood in New Orleans and
New Orleans East after Hurricane Katrina

**top:** Flooded city, Katrina 2005
**bottom left to right:** High-ground ridge, 1927 flood;
Katrina 2005: levee breach, flooded street, highway high ground

The ecology and phytogeography of New Orleans East is of the utmost importance to the survival of Wetland City. The density of the city relies on an aqua-urbanism that not only is protected by reconstructed wetlands and new artificial wetlands but is also sustained by the agri- and aqua-culture of the fresh- and saltwater wetlands. Since MRGO has destabilized the salinity content of Lake Pontchartrain, thereby increasing salinity content at the mouth of the Industrial Canal—where salt content should be, like that of the rest of the lake, significantly lower—its filling in is of utmost importance to the health of the local ecologies. (And that is not to mention the importance of this action to the safety of the people of New Orleans.) When this project is completed and MRGO becomes MRGONE Park and a linear storm buffer, the phytogeography can return to a highly diverse freshwater marsh to the north and a saltwater wetland to the south, reinstating a productive aqua-culture.

Also in the first infrastructural phase of this project, the neighborhood's existing political structure is extended along the major existing north–south boulevards into a neglected industrial swath of land between Chef Menteur Highway and MRGO. This area is intensely planted to remediate current industrial degradation in the short term (twenty-five to thirty years), and six long land bridges are constructed perpendicular to MRGONE Park. The new sustainable flood- and storm-resistant neighborhoods—Wilson Avenue, Crowder Boulevard,

Bundy Road, Read Boulevard, Wright Road, and Bullard Avenue—are built, and existing neighborhoods in New Orleans East are provided with rescue and community programs and clean, public transit systems.

Land-bridge neighborhoods follow the intelligence of the region's original system of land division, called the Arpent system. In this structure, established by French colonists in the eighteenth century, long, thin parcels run perpendicular to a river or stream like the Mississippi or Atchafalaya rivers and allow for a small frontage for every property. In this way, the main infrastructure sustains all the members of the system. Wetland City adopts this configuration with long, thin neighborhoods that attach to two infrastructures, the Chef Menteur Highway to the north and the new MRGONE Park to the south.

During the first phase of Wetland City, the levees along Lake Pontchartrain are maintained; but by 2050, which is the second phase, their upkeep is unaffordable, they are dismantled, and only high grounds are habitable in New Orleans East. At this point, the new aqua-urbanism of Wetland City is in full swing. Dense neighborhoods of varying programmatic focus, west to east, are established, as well as dense housing, productive recreational green systems, transit hubs and rescue stations, energy-producing artificial-wetland islands, and the Wetlands International Protection Institute (WIPI), which reuses three defunct highway interchanges in the protected Bayou Sauvage.

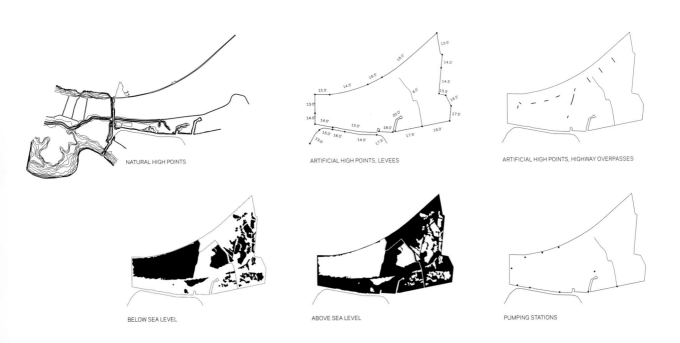

NATURAL HIGH POINTS

ARTIFICIAL HIGH POINTS, LEVEES

ARTIFICIAL HIGH POINTS, HIGHWAY OVERPASSES

BELOW SEA LEVEL

ABOVE SEA LEVEL

PUMPING STATIONS

Existing artificial and natural high and low points

top left: Highway and high ground in New Orleans East's major east–west roadways

top right: Section through New Orleans East with MRGO in its present form, Section through New Orleans East with MRGO reconfigured as MRGONE Park

middle and bottom: Arpent-system diagrams: elongated land division provides access to the Mississippi River for transport; any spinal organization can provide access to linear infrastructures

NEIGHBORHOOD POLITICAL DIVISIONS

DENSITY, ROADS, AND WETLANDS

RESIDENTIAL AND COMMERCIAL PATTERNS

RESIDENTIAL SETTLEMENT PATTERNS

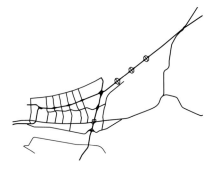

HIGHWAYS AND MAJOR ROADWAYS

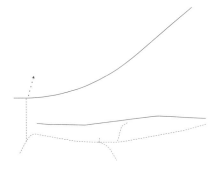

RAIL, WATER, AIR CIRCULATION

WETLANDS

WETLANDS AND OTHER GREEN SPACE

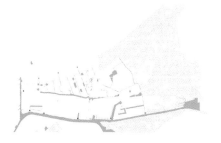

WETLANDS, WATERWAYS, AND PUMP STATIONS

New Orleans East, 2005

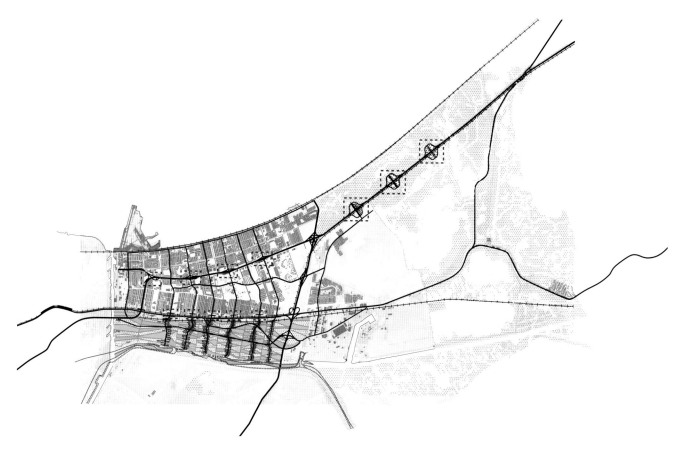

WETLAND CITY, 2025

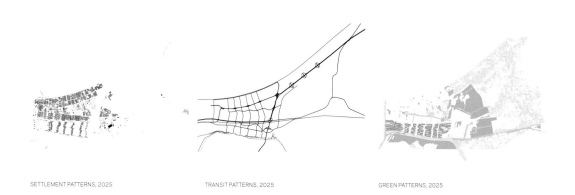

SETTLEMENT PATTERNS, 2025

TRANSIT PATTERNS, 2025

GREEN PATTERNS, 2025

New Orleans East, 2025

Since there will be less land for habitation, we propose a system of housing and neighborhood formations called Zydeco urbanism and Zydeco housing. This type of block and lot structure proposes that the current state of sprawl be squeezed, like the local musical instrument, into denser configurations. For example, sixty-four houses in a four-block area (the typical New Orleans East block layout) can be squeezed into one Zydeco block, increasing density fourfold and protecting three times the amount of land.

Zydeco housing is defined by its density and porosity. Promoting airflow and shading, the forms of the housing scheme stack on top of one another, opening holes for outdoor living at the street and upper levels. This scheme uses a thin-parcel structure, much like the Arpent system of land division, and attenuates the housing agglomerations along the length of the lot. Beginning at tall stacked forms, the multiple housing units descend as they move back into the lot, creating outbuildings, garages, workshops, and recreational buildings. This stepping configuration allows all the units to have views to the wetlands between neighborhood fingers.

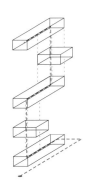

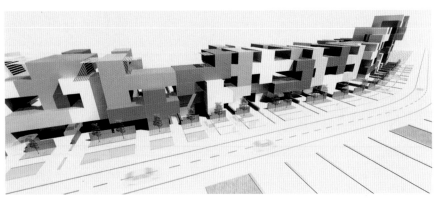

**top, left to right:** Zydeco housing diagrams: Unit elevational types, Modules
**middle and bottom left:** Perspective views of rear and front of Zydeco housing system
**right:** Plan of Zydeco housing system

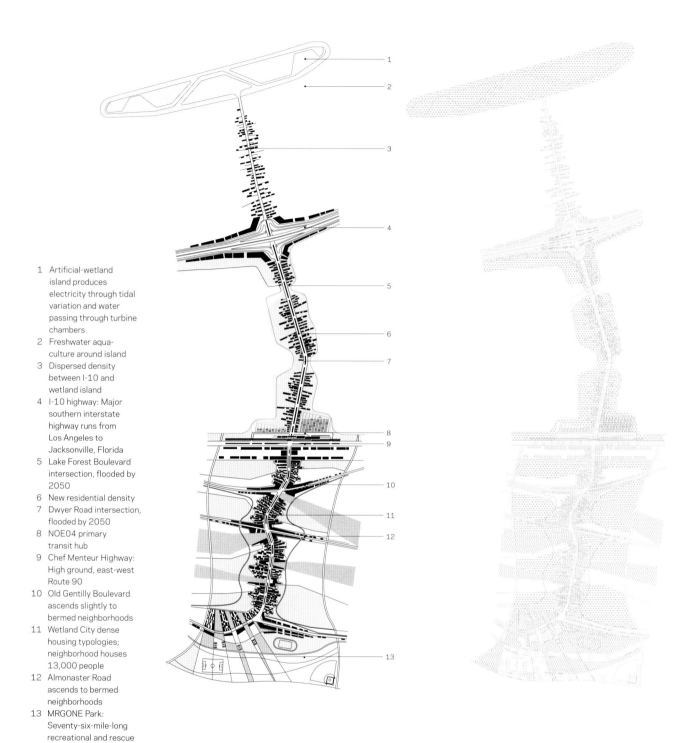

1 Artificial-wetland island produces electricity through tidal variation and water passing through turbine chambers

2 Freshwater aquaculture around island

3 Dispersed density between I-10 and wetland island

4 I-10 highway: Major southern interstate highway runs from Los Angeles to Jacksonville, Florida

5 Lake Forest Boulevard intersection, flooded by 2050

6 New residential density

7 Dwyer Road intersection, flooded by 2050

8 NOE04 primary transit hub

9 Chef Menteur Highway: High ground, east-west Route 90

10 Old Gentilly Boulevard ascends slightly to bermed neighborhoods

11 Wetland City dense housing typologies; neighborhood houses 13,000 people

12 Almonaster Road ascends to bermed neighborhoods

13 MRGONE Park: Seventy-six-mile-long recreational and rescue conduit; filled-in and raised high ground; filled with land and concrete that is beginning to be inundated with rising water levels

Wetland City density, 2105
**left:** Read Boulevard neighborhood settlement
**right:** Green pattern systems
(Programs at New Orleans East Wetland City are primarily institutional and recreational and residential. MRGONE Park becomes a scenic corridor for biking and hiking down to the Mississippi Delta, as well as a rescue conduit for St. Bernard Parish and New Orleans East.)

Between each linear neighborhood is a dense, productive green infrastructure of wetland agri- and aqua-culture, a continuation of public open space in the neighborhoods, and bioswales that remediate waste and process gray water. This green density, between the neighborhood berms, begins in the south at MRGONE Park and continues as far as possible toward the Chef Menteur Highway. Providing food and open space, interstitial wetlands protect against flooding and storm surges.

To establish a public transportation system for New Orleans East, this proposal latches onto a pre-Katrina light-rail plan that the city had considered. In this plan, a light-rail line was to run along the Chef Menteur Highway to the suburbs. In the new transit system, light-rails parallel bike and pedestrian paths, clean-fuel buses serve the north-south spines, and transit stations double as rescue centers. These stations formalize the hybrid light-rail and rescue system by creating buildings with similar programs, methods of site occupation, construction, palettes, and graphics. The primary hub station, NOE04, occupies the intersection of Chef Menteur Highway and Read Boulevard and comprises a light-rail station, bus station, bike-rental and repair shop, car parking and electric auto plug-in stations, and rescue-boat storage on the roof. NOE04, like all other stations, is constructed of precast parking-garage panels with integral beams. The panels are perforated to allow light and airflow and are supported by a field of steel columns with U-brackets into which the integral beams are nested. The precast panels can be delivered by flatbed railcar on the light-rail line. The field of columns extends into the parking area, and each column has a light fixture attached to its top. At night this fixture provides illumination; and in a flood, the lighting intensifies so that residents and rescue helicopters can locate it.

For clean energy production, a series of artificial-wetland islands are constructed in Lake Pontchartrain off the north shoreline of the current New Orleans East. These islands produce electricity through using tidal variation and water passing through turbine chambers, thereby enabling the industries, businesses, and residences of Wetland City to operate on clean, local energy. In addition, the islands promote freshwater aqua-culture and protect the area from storm surges off the lake.

Wetlands International Protection Institute (WIPI)

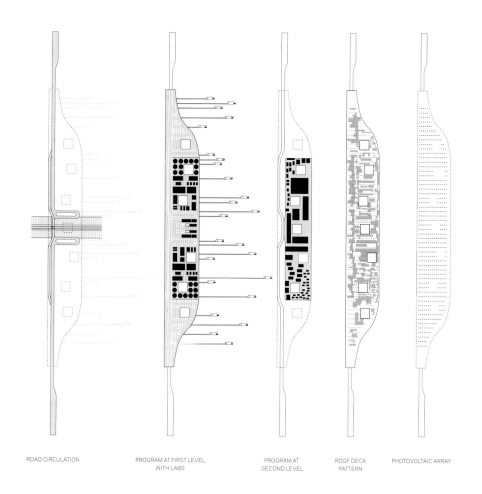

ROAD CIRCULATION  PROGRAM AT FIRST LEVEL WITH LABS  PROGRAM AT SECOND LEVEL  ROOF DECK PATTERN  PHOTOVOLTAIC ARRAY

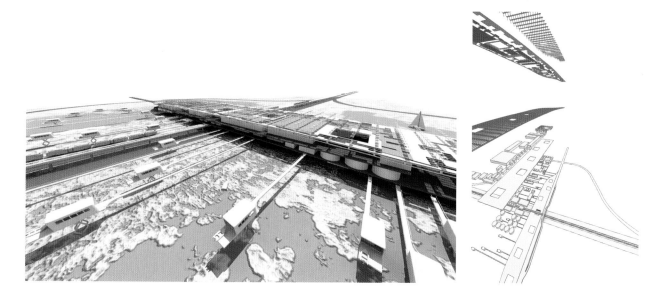

top: Plans
bottom left: Rendered view across labs, roof deck, and photovoltaic array
bottom right: Pulled-apart view of WIPI: (top to bottom) photovoltaic array, roof deck,
classrooms, cafe, library, visitors' center, mechanical systems, parking, light-rail station,
highway deck, light-rail tracks, I-10

Since this proposal is predicated on the reconstruction and preservation of wetlands, an institute is established, in Bayou Sauvage—the protected and often-infringed-upon wetland area to the east of New Orleans East—to study and reinforce these resources. The Wetlands International Protection Institute (WIPI) occupies three highway overpasses that were originally built in the Bayou to provide access to proposed suburban development. The Bayou was subsequently protected, but other wetlands in the Gulf region have continued to be destroyed. WIPI is established to protect wetlands and build awareness about wetlands issues; it uses the decks of the I-10 highway overpasses as existing high ground, which, by 2050, will hover over water and reestablished wetlands. The institute buildings occupy the first overpass to the west and include a visitor center, residences, classrooms, and laboratories. The other two overpasses function as field labs and outposts for the study of aqua-culture study.

Through these projects and this phased process, Wetland City is one hundred percent aqua-urban.

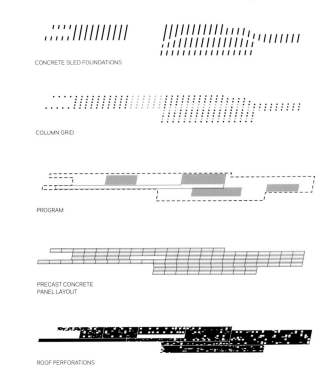

CONCRETE SLED FOUNDATIONS

COLUMN GRID

PROGRAM

PRECAST CONCRETE
PANEL LAYOUT

ROOF PERFORATIONS

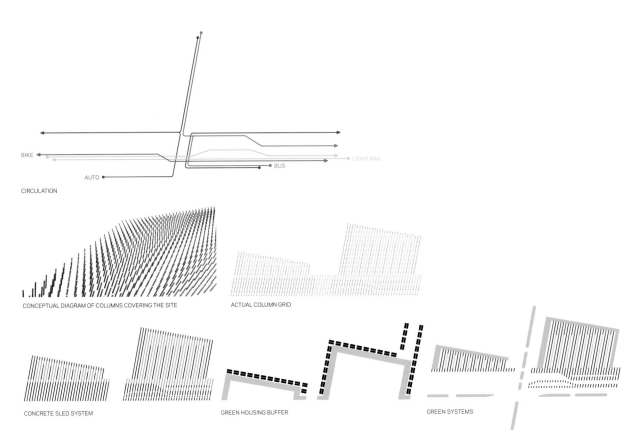

BIKE

LIGHT RAIL

AUTO                    BUS

CIRCULATION

CONCEPTUAL DIAGRAM OF COLUMNS COVERING THE SITE

ACTUAL COLUMN GRID

CONCRETE SLED SYSTEM

GREEN HOUSING BUFFER

GREEN SYSTEMS

**top:** NOE04 plans of building components
**bottom:** Site plan components

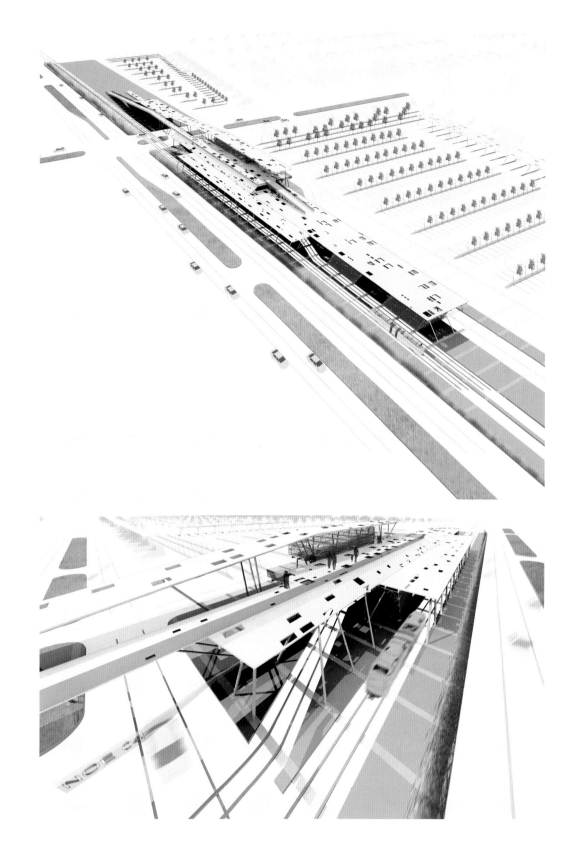

top: NOE04 transit hub: Southeast rendered view from southeast and above
bottom: Rendered view along tracks

NOE04 rendered view with Coast Guard helicopter landing on roof

PRECAST CONCRETE DECKS DELIVERED
ON FLATBED TRUCK

PRECAST CONCRETE FOUNDATION

STEEL COLUMNS

PRECAST CONCERET DECKS

top: NOE04 rendered view inside station
bottom: Construction assembly system

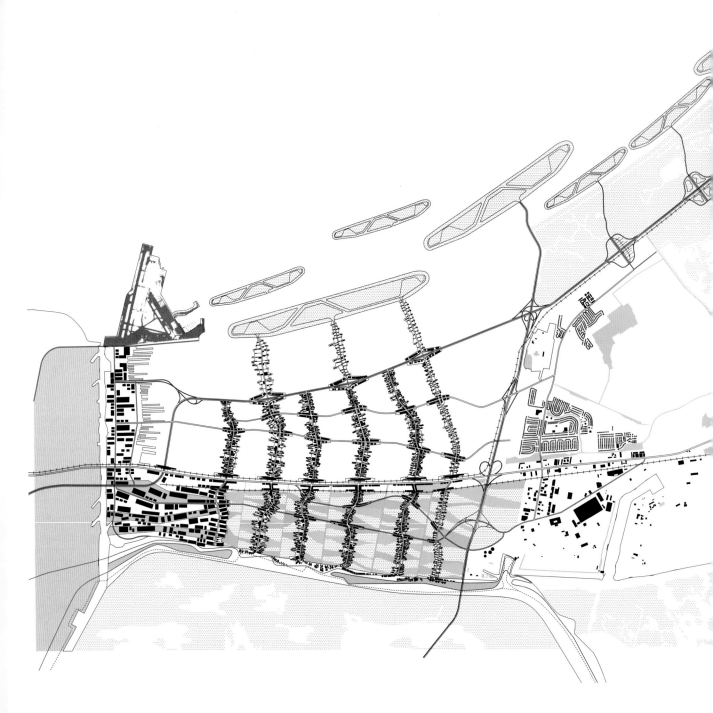

Wetland City 2105

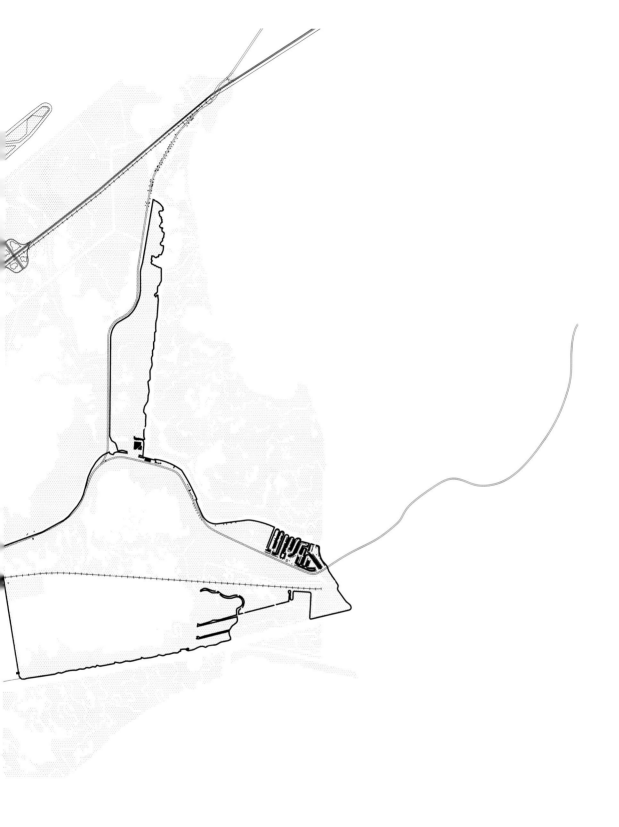

**Appendix**

# Leven Betts Furniture

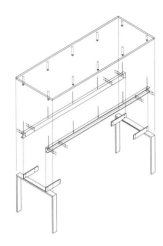

**Light-rail table:** one-inch sanded acrylic (top);
three-inch steel channel on steel flat-bar legs (base);
powder-coated charcoal gray (finish);
84" L x 30" W x 30" H (dimensions)

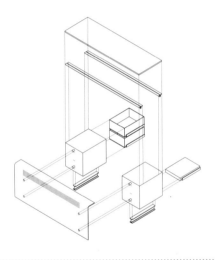

**Magnetar:** solid black synthetic surface (desktop);
sanded acrylic with stainless-steel drawers (file cabinets);
anodized-aluminum screen (structural components);
84" L x 30" W x 37" H (dimensions)

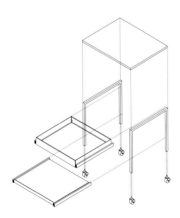

**Side light:** three-quarter-inch sanded acrylic (top);
brushed and lacquered cold-rolled steel tube and hot-rolled
steel channels (frame); brushed and lacquered aluminum
with exposed drawer slides (drawer and tray);
24" L x 20" W x 20" H (dimensions)

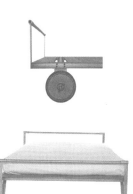

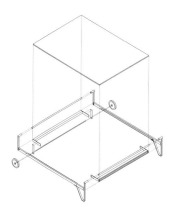

**Bed of rails:** steel flat bar, angle, and tube (frame);
ten-inch-diameter locking wheels;
Baltic birch (mattress support);
powder-coated light gray (finish);
6' 8" L x 4' 8" W x 20" H (dimensions)

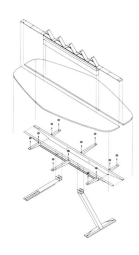

**Ironing board-room table:** one-inch-sanded acrylic (top);
powder-coated steel (base); stainless-steel housing
for electrical and data outlets (power strip);
120" L (varies) x 60" W x 30" H (dimensions)

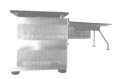

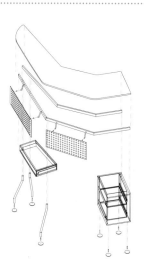

**Wing:** solid black synthetic surface (top);
sanded acrylic with stainless-steel drawers (file cabinet
and pencil-drawer box); powder-coated steel (legs and frame);
perforated stainless steel (screens); black plastic levelers (feet);
120" L x 30" W x 30" H (dimensions)

# Other Projects

**Princeton House**
2007 DESIGN PHASE

**Tribeca Penthouse**
2007 UNDER CONSTRUCTION

**Brooklyn Townhouse**
2007 UNDER CONSTRUCTION

**Syracuse Exhibition**
2007

Tribeca Townhouse
2007

Columbia County House Renovation
2007

Manhattan Ave Roof Addition
2007

East 97th Street Townhouse
2006

**Guadalajara Library**
2006

**Long Island House Addition**
2006

**Brooklyn Loft**
2005

**East Hampton House**
2007

**Sublime Furniture Showroom**
2004

**SoHo Loft**
2003

**ABDC Dance Studio**
2002

**Madison Square Loft**
1998

# Project Credits

**CC01 House: Columbia County, NY**
Project Team: David Leven, Stella Betts, Tim Furzer,
    Andrew Feuerstein, Jonathan Man, Rachel Chaos
Structural Engineer: Nat Oppenheimer, Robert Silman
    Associates
General Contractor: Leven Betts
Carpentry Contractor: Scott Dean
Photograph of Model: Andrew Zuckerman
Photographer: Michael Moran

**Catskills House: Stone Ridge, NY**
Project Team: David Leven, Stella Betts, Tim Furzer,
    Matthew Corsover, Jorge Fontan, John Young
Structural Engineer: Nat Oppenheimer, Robert Silman
    Associates
Contractor: Eric Glasser
Builder: Raphael Ben Yehuda
Photograph of Model: Andrew Zuckerman
Photographer: Michael Moran

**VVE House: Hurley, NY**
Project Team: David Leven, Stella Betts, Christian Eusebio,
    Andrew Feuerstein, Rachel Johnston
Photograph of Model: Andrew Zuckerman

**Chelsea Penthouse: New York, NY**
Project Team: David Leven, Stella Betts
Contractor: American Woodworking Construction
Photographer: Elizabeth Felicella

**Cedarhurst Spiral Housing: Cedarhurst, NY**
Project Team: David Leven, Stella Betts, Andrew Feuerstein

**Nassau Street Lobby: New York, NY**
Project Team: David Leven, Stella Betts
Contractor: J + S Design Construction
Photographer: Elizabeth Felicella

**Mixed Greens Gallery: New York, NY**
Project Team: David Leven, Stella Betts, Tim Furzer,
    Jonathan Man, Rachel Chaos
Interior Designer: Ghislaine Vinas Interior Design
Lighting Designer: Suzan Tillotson, Tillotson Design
    Associates

Structural Engineer: Nat Oppenheimer, Robert Silman
    Associates
Code Consultant: Joe DeCeglie, William Vitacco Associates
Construction Manager: Taocon Inc
Photograph of Model: Andrew Zuckerman
Photographer: Michael Moran

**Stockholm Public Library Addition: Stockholm, Sweden**
Project Team: David, Leven, Stella Betts, Jean Luc Torchon,
    Kibur Sahlu, Lucas Echeveste, Erica Quinones, Christian
    Eusebio, Mathias Christensen, Sara Camre, Rachel
    Johnston, Trudy Giordano, Rachel Chaos
Photograph of Model: Andrew Zuckerman
Structural Engineer: Nat Oppenheimer, Robert Silman
    Associates

**Les Migrateurs Furniture Showroom: New York, NY**
Project Team: David Leven, Stella Betts
Structural Engineer: Nat Oppenheimer, Robert Silman
    Associates
Code Consultant: Calibre Building Consultants
Contractor: E + A Construction
Photographer: Elizabeth Felicella

**EMR Printing Plant: New York, NY**
Project Team: David Leven, Stella Betts
Structural Engineer: Trevor Salmon
Mechanical / Electrical Engineer: HHF Design
Code Consultation: Calibre Building Consultants
Construction Manager: Taocon Inc
Photographer: Elizabeth Felicella

**Site Lines: Parsons the New School for Design,
    New York, NY**
Project Team: David Leven, Stella Betts, Tim Furzer,
    Andrew Feuerstein, Jonathan Man, Rachel Chaos
Metal Framing Studs: Donation from Taocon Inc
Parsons Students: Parker Lee, Kip Katich, Christian Eusebio,
    Nancy Kim, Lindsey Farrell

**Line Weights: University of Texas, Austin, TX**
Project Team: David Leven, Stella Betts. Tim Furzer,
    Andrew Feuerstein, Jonathan Man, Rachel Chaos
UT Austin Student: Ben Arbib

Piranesi as Designer: Cooper-Hewitt National Design
    Museum, New York, NY
Project Team: David Leven, Stella Betts, Lucas Echeveste,
    Andrew Feuerstein, Christian Eusebio, Trudy Giordano,
    Rachel Johnston, Nick Na
Co-curators: Dr. Sarah E. Lawrence, John Wilton-Ely
Graphic Designer: Tsang Seymour Design
Lighting Designer: Mary Ann Hoag

Frederic Church, Winslow Homer, and Thomas Moran:
    Tourism and the American Landscape: Cooper-Hewitt
    National Design Museum, New York, NY
Project Team: David Leven, Stella Betts, Tim Furzer,
    Jonathan Man, Andrew Feuerstein
Curator: Gail S. Davidson
Graphic Designer: Tsang Seymour Design
Lighting Designer: Jeffery Nash

Filter Parking
Project Team: David Leven, Stella Betts

Chicago Filter Park: Chicago, IL
Project Team: David Leven, Stella Betts, Matthew Corsover
Structural Engineer: Nat Oppenheimer, Robert Silman
    Associates
Photograph of Model: Andrew Zuckerman

Greenwich Street Park Apartments: New York, NY
Project Team: David Leven, Stella Betts, Tim Furzer

Spaces Between the Hills: Ramallah / Jerusalem /
    Bethlehem
Project Team: David Leven, Stella Betts, David Snyder,
    Andrew Feuerstein
Editor: Michael Sorkin

Wetland City: New Orleans East Urban Proposal
Project Team: David Leven, Stella Betts, Yulia Ilizarov,
    Andrew Feuerstein, Jean Luc Torchon, Rachel Johnston,
    Chris Soohoo, Christian Eusebio

# Selected Bibliography

## 2008

"Mixed Greens Gallery," *Illuminate Magazine* (January 2008), 22-25.

McDonald, Shannon S., ed. *The Parking Garage: Design and Evolution of a Modern Urban Form*. Washington, DC: Urban Land Institute, 2008.

## 2007

"Design Vanguard 2007," *Architectural Record*, (December 2007), 74-77.

Engelhorn, Beate, ed. *Young Americans: New Architecture in the USA*. Berlin: Dom Publishers, 2007.

"Mixed Greens Gallery," *Interior World* 61 (November 2007), 136-143.

Sanchez Vidiella, Alex, ed. *Atlas of Office Interiors*. Barcelona: LOFT Publications, 2007.

Sanchez Vidiella, Alex, ed. *Minimal: The Big Book of Minimalism*. Barcelona: LOFT Publications, 2007.

Yelavich, Susan, ed. *Contemporary World Interiors*. London: Phaidon Press Limited, 2007.

## 2006

"Going Slightly Green." *Frame* 50 (May/June 2006). Mixed Greens Gallery.

Llorella, Anja, ed. *New Minimalists Houses*. New York: Harper Collins Publisher, 2006. CC01 House.

Llorella, Anja, ed. *Ultimate New York Design*. New York: teNeues Publishing Company, 2006. Mixed Greens Gallery

"Mixed Greens." *Architectural Record* (August 2006). Mixed Greens Gallery.

"Mixed Greens Gallery: Conceptual Transformation." *DisenArt* (August 2006). Mixed Greens Gallery.

"Play It As It Lays." *Dwell* (September 2006). CC01 House.

## 2005

"Landscape Portrait." *Surface* (November 2005). Catskills House and CC01 House.

"Looks Can Be Deceiving." *Interior Design* (November 2005). Mixed Greens Gallery.

## 2004

"Annual Design Review 2004: Filter Park," *I.D. Magazine*, (July-August 2004), 178.

"Auto Show." *Metropolis* (February 2004). Chicago Filter Park

"Focus on Retail Interiors." *Architectural Record* (February 2004). Sublime Furniture Showroom.

"Patriot Act." *Metropolis* (June 2004). Sublime Furniture Showroom.

"RAW: Metropolis Next Generation Prize." *Metropolis* (May 2004). Filter Parking.

"What's In Store." *Elle Décor* (February/March 2004). Sublime Furniture Showroom.

*Young Architects 5*. New York: Princeton Architectural Press, 2004. Various projects.

## 2003

*Inspired Retail Space*. Beverly, MA: Rockport Publishers, 2003. Les Migrateurs Furniture Showroom.

"No Little Plan." *Competitions* (Fall 2003). Chicago Prize, Stop Go Chicago Portal Project.

"Sublime." *Surface* (October 2003). Sublime Furniture Showroom.

"Vehicular Visions." *Chicago Reader* (June 27, 2003). Chicago Filter Park.

## 2002

Betts, Stella, David Leven, and David Snyder. "Spaces Between the Hills." *The Next Jerusalem: Sharing the Divided City*. Ed. Michael Sorkin. New York: Monacelli Press, 2002. An urban design proposal for the region of Jerusalem.

"Outside In." *Metropolis* (June 2002). Chelsea Penthouse.

## 2001

Coleman, Cindy, ed. *Interior Design Handbook for Professional Practice*. New York: McGraw Hill Publishers, 2001. EMR Printing Plant.

## 2000

"Special Delivery." *Interior Design* (November 2000). EMR Printing Plant.

## 1999

"Plastic Fantastic." *House and Garden* (February 1999). Kitchen Renovation.

# Professional Notes

David Leven was born in Washington, D.C., in 1964. He is a partner at Leven Betts Architects and director of the Graduate Architecture Program at Parsons the New School for Design. He holds a BA from Colgate University and an MArch from Yale University and attended the Institute for Architecture and Urban Studies. He is a registered architect in the states of New York and New Jersey.

Stella Betts was born in Phoenix, Arizona, in 1966. She is a partner at Leven Betts Architects and is an adjunct professor at Parsons the New School for Design, where she coordinates the graduate thesis studio. She holds a BA from Connecticut College and an MArch from Harvard University.

David and Stella founded Leven Betts Architects in 1997. The firm has received numerous awards, including four AIA awards, an Architectural Record Design Vanguard Award, an ID Annual Design Review Award, a New York Foundation for the Arts Grant, and the firm was recognized in the Young Architects Forum in 2003. David and Stella live in New York City.

## Awards and Honors

New York Foundation for the Arts Grant, 2008.

Design Merit Award, AIA New York Chapter, Stockholm Public Library Addition, 2008.

Winner, Design Vanguard, International Portfolio Competition, *Architectural Record,* 2008.

Notable Projects, Workplace, *Architype Review* Award, Mixed Greens Gallery, 2007.

Award of Merit, IES New York City Section Lumen Award, Mixed Greens Gallery, 2006.

Design Merit Award, Interior Architecture, AIA New York Chapter, Mixed Greens Gallery, 2005.

Design Honor Award, Project, AIA New York Chapter, Greenwich Street Park Apartments, 2004.

Artists in Residence, MacDowell Colony Fellows, Peterborough, NH, 2004.

Design Distinction, Concepts, *I.D.* Annual Design Review, Chicago Filter Park, 2004.

Runner-up, Next Generation Prize, *Metropolis,* Filter Parking, 2004.

Design Honor Award, Project, AIA New York Chapter, Chicago Filter Park, 2003.

First Prize, International Design Competition, Chicago Prize, Chicago Filter Park, 2003.

Winner, Young Architects Forum, National Portfolio Competition, Architectural League of New York, 2003.

Third Prize, AD House Competition, 2002.

Finalist, *Architectural Record/Business Week* Competition, EMR Printing Plant, 2000.

## Exhibitions

AIA 2008 Design Awards, New York Center for Architecture, New York, NY, 2008; Berlin-New York Dialogues: Building in Context, German Center for Architecture DAZ, Berlin, Germany, 2007; Berlin-New York Dialogues: Building in Context, New York Center for Architecture, New York, NY, 2007; Pattern Recognition, Syracuse University School of Architecture, Syracuse, NY, 2007; Young Americans, Deutsches Architekturmuseum, Frankfurt, Germany, 2007; Line Weights, University of Texas, Austin, TX, 2006; Site Lines, Parsons the New School for Design, New York, NY, 2006; AIA Design Award: Mixed Greens Gallery, Center for Architecture, New York, NY, 2005; AIA Design Award: Greenwich Street Park Apartments, Center for Architecture, New York, NY, 2004; Metropolis NEXT: Filter Parking, Center for Architecture, New York, NY, 2004; RAW Exhibition, Metropolis Next Generation Prize: Filter Parking, ICFF, New York, NY, 2004; AIA Design Award: Chicago Filter Park, Center for Architecture, New York, NY, 2003; Chicago Prize: Chicago Filter Park, Chicago City Hall, Chicago, IL, 2003; Chicago Prize: Chicago Filter Park, Chicago Institute of Art, Chicago, IL, 2003; Young Architects Award Exhibition, Architectural League of New York, New York, NY, 2003; AD House Competition: Traveling Exhibition of Winning Entries, Kulturgeschichtliches Museum, Osnabrueck, Germany and; Bruckenthal Museum, Sibiu, Romania, 2003.

## Lectures

Syracuse University, Syracuse, NY, 2007; University of Kansas, Lawrence, KS, 2006; University of Texas, Austin, TX, 2006; Parsons the New School for Design, New York, NY, 2006; AIAS Emerging Lecture, Pratt School of Design, New York, NY, 2005; Architectural League of New York, New York, NY, 2004; Annual Board of Directors Meeting, MacDowell Colony, Peterborough, NH, 2004; Architectural League of New York, New York, NY, 2003; Boston Architectural Center, Boston, MA, 2003; Colgate University, Hamilton, NY, 2002.

# Employees

# Acknowledgments

Since the production of architecture is a collective act, there are many collaborators to whom we are forever indebted. We are particularly grateful to all who have comprised our office staff at one time or another and have helped us draw, model, and build our work. We also thank our clients, collaborators in a very special sense, most of whose projects are represented in the pages of this book. Most notably, Raphael ben Yehuda, Eric Reinitz, Henry Personnaz, Greg Miller and Jim Godfrey, and the whole Birbil clan trusted us with key projects that enabled us to further the purview of our work. We would also like to thank the consultants and builders who have gone beyond the parameters of duty and contract to help us marry the pragmatic with the adventurous in our work, particularly our structural engineer Nat Oppenheimer of Robert Silman Associates; our lighting designer Suzan Tillotson; interior designer, Ghislaine Vinas; and Steve Lamazor, Jon Fogler, and everyone at Taocon Inc, who have always been willing to wrap their heads around challenging construction scenarios, often under severe schedules, and to execute our work at the highest degrees of finish, quality, and integrity.

A number of professional photographers have photographed our work, and we are forever indebted to them as they capture aspects of our projects that are important to us and always go farther to create singular images. Michael Moran hones in on our architectural intentions through his insight, powers of perception, composition, and patience; Elizabeth Felicella shot many of our early projects with a keen eye for detail and light; and Andrew Zuckerman, always eager to engage the forms and ideas of our work in film, also operates as an incisive adviser.

We must also recognize the editors and writers of various magazines, books, and journals who have included us in the discussion of contemporary architectural and urban design issues that their publications promote. These individuals include Mayer Rus, Susan Szenazy, Martin Pedersen, Cliff Pearson, Philip Noble, Aric Chen, Susan Yelavich, Beate Engelhorn, Michael Sorkin, and Kevin Lippert and Jennifer Thompson (more about them later).

Several institutions have supported us. We would like to thank the MacDowell Colony for giving us time and space to work; and the Architectural League, especially Rosalie Genevro and Anne Reiselbach, for catapulting us forward with our inclusion in several key public programs; the New York Foundation for the Arts for honoring us with a NYFA grant; and the Graham Foundation.

We are grateful to the students and colleagues of the schools where we have taught—Parsons the New School for Design, the City College of New York, and Syracuse University—for engaging us in the pursuit of architectural ideas. We also thank the leaders of those programs, Peter Wheelwright, Kent Kleinman, David Lewis, George Ranalli, and Mark Robbins, for including us in the debates about architecture at their schools as well as promoting our pedagogy and practice.

We are indebted to a number of friends and colleagues for their support, advice, and patience during the writing of this book and the trajectory of our architectural production, in particular Hanneline Rogeberg and Zach Rockhill, who deserve a special thanks for their unfailing support and inquisitiveness into our work and lives; and David Snyder, a lifelong collaborator and dear friend who has forced us to engage architecture at levels well beyond the boundaries of our practice. We must also thank K. Michael Hays, for his support; George Wagner, for his uncanny insight; and Michael Sorkin, one of the few mentors we've ever had, for inspiring us not only with his humor, genius, and critical stance but also with his openness to take us and our work seriously at times when we might not have.

We are also thankful to Ron, Leslie, Steve, and Eric Leven, Janet Cooper, Rose and Bill Leven, and Charles, Petra, Paul, Sylvie, Lucie, and Anna Betts who have instilled in us the love of design and have given us the support and space (even when it might have been difficult to understand why architecture requires so much space and time) to pursue our work. We are particularly grateful to Paul Betts for his insights into issues of design, history, and the presentation (and utter importance) of one's ideas and work.

For the specific tasks related to the making of this book, we would like to thank Jean Luc Torchon and Yuliya Ilizarov, as well as Andrew Feuerstein for his contributions to the book and his tireless commitment to the work. Finally, we are grateful to Kevin Lippert and Jennifer Thompson, whose guidance, advice, and cuisine made the process of compiling our first book less uncertain and more pleasurable than we could have imagined. We would also like to extend our thanks to everyone at Princeton Architectural Press who made this book happen.

Graham Foundation / Princeton Architectural Press series
New Voices in Architecture presents first monographs on emerging
designers from around the world

Published by
Princeton Architectural Press
37 East 7th Street, New York, New York 10003

For a free catalog of books, call 1-800-722-6657
Visit our website at www.papress.com

Editor: Jennifer N. Thompson
Designer: Paul Wagner

Special thanks to: Nettie Aljian, Sara Bader, Dorothy Ball, Nicola Bednarek,
Janet Behning, Becca Casbon, Carina Cha, Penny (Yuen Pik) Chu,
Russell Fernandez, Pete Fitzpatrick, Wendy Fuller, Jan Haux,
Clare Jacobson, Aileen Kwun, Nancy Eklund Later, Linda Lee, Aaron Lim,
Laurie Manfra, Katharine Myers, Ceara O'Leary, Lauren Nelson Packard,
Arnoud Verhaeghe, Joseph Weston, and Deb Wood of
Princeton Architectural Press —Kevin C. Lippert, publisher

Library of Congress Cataloging-in-Publication Data
Leven, David, 1964–
Leven Betts : pattern recognition / David Leven and Stella Betts ;
with an introduction by Michael Sorkin.
     p.     cm.
ISBN 978-1-56898-782-8 (alk. paper)
1. Leven Betts (Firm) 2. Architecture—United States—21st century.
I. Betts, Stella, 1966- II. Title.
NA737.L4527L48 2008
720.973—dc22
                                    2008019130

Image Credits

p. 52:
Jacques Tati, *Playtime*, 1967: photo courtesy of Photofest, Inc.

pp. 117–120:
Piranesi as Designer
All exhibition installation photos and renderings © 2006
Smithsonian Institution
Rijksmuseum, Amsterdam, the Netherlands
The Pierpont Morgan Library, New York
Minneapolis Institute of Arts
Sir John Soane's Museum, London
Powerhouse Museum
Victoria and Albert Museum
Leeds Art Galleries, Lotherton Hall

pp. 124–127:
Frederic Church, Winslow Homer, and Thomas Moran: Tourism
and the American Landscape
All exhibition installation photos and renderings © 2006
Smithsonian Institution

p. 124, images within bottom left:
Trade card: *The Only Route via Niagara Falls & Suspension Bridge:
Take the Great Western and Michigan Central R.W. Line*
Published by Clay, Cosack & Co.
Buffalo, NY, late nineteenth century
Chromolithograph on white wove paper
Warshaw Collection of Business Americana-Railroads,
Archives Center, National Museum of American History,
Behring Center, Smithsonian Institution
—
Trade card: *The Only Route via Niagara Falls: Take the Michigan
Central from Chicago*
Published by Shober and Carqueville
Chicago, IL, late nineteenth century
Chromolithograph on cream wove paper
Warshaw Collection of Business Americana-Railroads,
Archives Center, National Museum of American History,
Behring Center, Smithsonian Institution
—
Ferdinand Richardt (Austrian, 1819-1895)
*Niagara*, ca. 1855
Oil on canvas
Lent by Heckscher Museum of Art, Huntington, New York,
August Heckscher Collection
—
Photograph: *Power Stations below Niagara Falls*
United States, August 15, 1906
Gelatin silver print
Lent by the New York Historical Society

p. 131:
Aerial Photos: photos courtesy of Photovault

p. 161:
New Orleans Flood Photos
AP Wide World Photos
University of Chicago Special Collections Library